KITCHEN LIBRARY

FISH &
SHELLFISH

KITCHEN LIBRARY

FISH & SHELLFISH

Edited by Susan Spaull

GREENWICH
EDITIONS

This edition published in 2005
by Greenwich Editions
The Chrysalis Building
Bramley Road, London W10 6SP

An imprint of **Chrysalis** Books Group plc

All correspondence concerning the content of this
volume should be addressed to Greenwich Editions.

Photographer: Philip Wilkins
Food stylist: Sue Spaull
Nutritional information: Jenny McGlyne
Editor: Katherine Edelston
Designer: Cara Hamilton
Reproduction: Anorax Imaging Ltd
Printed and bound in China

ISBN 0-86288-815-8

10 9 8 7 6 5 4 3 2 1

The publishers would like to thank the Fish Shop at
Kensington Place, London for supplying the wonderful
fish for the photographs.

Contents

Visual Index

Brill with Cardamom Fillets and rich sauce with roasted cardamom pods p29

Steamed Brill & Vegetables Light dish of steamed courgettes, leeks and celery with herbs p30

Sole with Mint & Cucumber Fillets poached in wine stock with a creamy sauce p33

Sole with Chive Sauce Prawns and rolled fillets in vermouth, chives and wine sauce p35

Sole with Lettuce Filling Steamed fillets with ricotta cheese, lettuce and leek filling p36

Plaice with Prosciutto Wrapped in strips of ham with sage leaves, perfect with pasta p39

Stuffed Sole Mushrooms, sun-dried tomatoes and anchovy paste for impact p41

Fish & Pesto Parcels Filo packages of salmon or turbot with prawns, mushrooms and pesto p42

Turbot Parcels Garlicky pepper sauce and spinach leaves for striking visual effect p43

Fish with Mushroom Crust Grilled chestnut mushroom topping with mustard p45

Turbot with Orange Sauce Ginger saffron and orange, great with grilled fennel p46

Halibut with Courgettes Paper parcels of baked halibut with sliced courgettes p48

Halibut with Paprika Strips of halibut with shiitake mushrooms, red pepper and a paprika kick p51

Yoghurt Topped Halibut Steaks with cumin, coriander, mint and paprika p53

Chowder Smoked and fresh haddock with prawns, potatoes and sweetcorn p55

Haddock & Parsley Sauce Forget the ready-made disappointment, the classic poached dish p56

Haddock with Tomatoes Piquant balance of tomatoes, Dijon mustard and chives p58

Cod with Teriyaki Glaze Grilled with soy sauce, ginger and brown sugar p61

Roast Cod with Lentils Green or brown lentils with coriander, tomatoes and saffron p62

Fish Cakes Mixed white and smoked fish, fine with an onion salad p64

Fish Gratins Cheshire or Cheddar cheese with Parmesan and Dijon mustard p65

Goujons with Piquant Dip Mayonnaise and yogurt dip with gherkins, mustard and capers p67

Hot Fish Loaf Terrine of white fish with prawns, enlivened with anchovy essence and cayenne p69

Whiting with Italian Sauce Pan-fried whiting with an onion, anchovy and parsley sauce p71

Sesame-Coated Whiting Grilled in a tarragon and Dijon mustard coating p72

Whiting with Spinach Button mushrooms, spinach, nutmeg and Parmesan p75

Monkfish in Coconut Cream South East Asian approach to monkfish tail with ginger, lemon grass and creamed coconut p76

Middle-Eastern Monkfish With cinnamon and caraway seeds, well matched with couscous p78

Chunky Fish Casserole White fish and prawns or mussels and clams with pasta p81

Monkfish on Ratatouille Aubergines, courgettes, peppers and tomatoes with herbs p82

Ceviche Monkfish or halibut with chilli and coriander, as an appetizer or main dish p84

Grilled Fish & Coriander Great with grey mullet, cumin, coriander, paprika and chilli p87

Hake Baked with Potatoes Hake cutlets baked with potatoes, red pepper and tomato p89

Red Snapper with Crostini Marinated in orange with fennel and anchovy fillets p90

Bream with Tarragon Also works with red mullet, a tarragon and tomato accompaniment p92

Sea Bass under a Crust Simply baked in a sea salt crust with fresh herbs p95

Sea Bass & Garlic Superb combination of bacon, thyme and onions p96

Bass with Ginger & Lime Eastern approach with Chinese sesame oil and soy sauce p98

Spiced Bass Marinade of ginger, grapeseed oil and Chinese five spice powder p100

Trout with Tomato Sauce Grilled fillets with a salsa of tomatoes, capers and herbs p101

Trout with Hazelnuts Fried and chopped hazelnuts and whole trout, perfect with a mixed leaf salad p102

Trout with Parma Ham Baked, wrapped in ham with sprigs of basil or tarragon p105

Tandoori Trout Garam masala, turmeric, chillies and cayenne for a taste of the subcontinent p107

Trout & Artichoke Frittata Wedges of flaked trout with sautéd artichoke p108

Mixed Fish Pot Red mullet, red snapper, bream or trout with monkfish or sea bass p111

Salmon with Avocado Salsa Chilli, coriander and lime juice salsa with tomato and avocado p112

Salmon with Herb Sauce Baked with wine and served with a watercress sauce p114

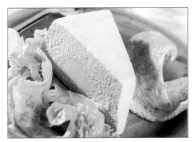

Salmon & Avocado Mousse A creamy combination, ideal with melba toast p116

Salmon Stir-Fry Asparagus and sesame oil, best served with egg noodles p119

Salmon Canapés Superior snacks with red salmon and paprika, garnished with avocado p120

Chinese Salad with Salmon Fried in groundnut oil with rice wine and beansprouts p123

Salmon Mousse The classic mousse with cucumber and a hint of paprika p125

Salmon Puffs Light mixture of salmon and olives in choux puffs p126

Layered Fish Terrine Elegant and creamy layers of salmon and white fish p128

Gravad Lax Traditional dill and mustard sauce with marinated salmon p131

Tuna Basquaise From Spain, tuna steaks with intense tomato and garlic flavour, p132

Warm Tuna Niçoise Justly famous combination of green beans, olives and anchovy p135

Tuna & Ginger Vinaigrette Lime, ginger and soy sauce flavours go well with peppers and leeks p137

Herrings in Oatmeal Grilled in oatmeal coating, served with a mustard sauce p138

Mackerel with Mustard Dijon mustard, fresh coriander and rolled oats p139

Mackerel with Yogurt Grilled with a spice mixture of harissa, cumin and garlic p141

Sardines in Coriander Sauce Lime rind and juice with toasted coriander seeds p142

Stuffed Sardines Filled with a herb mixture plus pine nuts and baked p144

Anchovy Beignets Anchovy and almond mixture, deep-fried and served as an appetizer p147

Spicy Fish Balls Canapés or appetizers with ginger, curry powder and sesame seeds p149

Sushi with Shrimp Bite-size packages of shrimp with rice flavoured with sweet sake and hot horseradish wasabi powder p150

John Dory with Orange John dory fillets baked with mint, orange rind and vermouth p152

Fish & Watercress Sauce
Watercress mayonnaise sauce with
John Dory or brill fillets p155

Bream Duglere Bream fillets in a
creamy white wine sauce with
tomato p156

Baked Bream with Fennel Baked
whole sea bream with fennel and
rosemary p159

Bream with Lemon & Herbs
Fillets baked in paper with fresh
herbs p161

Chinese Style Bream Soy sauce,
sesame and groundnut oil with
chillies, steamed p163

Fish Plaki A choice of whole fish
baked with celery, tomatoes and
coriander seeds in white wine p164

Skate with Anchovy Sauce Fried
skate wings with a sauce of capers
and herbs p166

Stir-Fried Squid Oriental-style
dish of lemon grass, rice wine and
ginger p169

Stuffed Squid Baby squid stuffed
with tomatoes and anchovies and
baked p170

Turkish Swordfish Kebabs
Marinated in paprika, with a
parsley and lemon sauce p173

Swordfish with Tomatoes Steaks
with intense flavour of sun-dried
tomatoes and black olives p175

Escabeche Marinade of saffron,
chilli, orange, cumin seeds and red
peppers p176

Cajun-Style Red Snapper
Blackened spicy coating of paprika, cayenne pepper and mustard p179

Red Snapper with Mushrooms
Mushrooms, coriander and tangy tangerine juice p181

Swordfish with Courgette Sauce
Pan fried swordfish with fried courgette and garlic sauce p182

Artichokes with Caviar Crispy rounds of bread topped with artichoke, sour cream, aioli, herbs and caviar p185

Caviar Croutons Sour cream and horseradish with red salmon caviar for a pretty canapé p186

Caviar Moulds Beautiful black caviar moulds, decorated with boiled egg p187

Celery with Shrimp Crisp celery rafts of shrimp with sour cream, capers and chives p189

Cantonese Prawns King prawns marinated in orange rind, honey and soy sauce p190

Grilled Prawns in Ginger Wine
Grilled and basted in a soy mixture with lemon juice p191

Shrimp Vol-au-Vents Spicy chopped prawns in vol-au-vent cases p193

Spanish Prawns Fiery chilli, garlic and prawns served with homemade tartar sauce p195

Prawns with Asian Sauce Marinade of basil, ginger, green chillies and rice wine p196

Baked Prawns & Courgettes Easy method for prawns, with oregano and Parmesan p199

Indian-Style Prawns Spicy prawns simmered in yogurt, mint and saffron p200

Shrimp Risotto Shallots, tarragon, saffron, prawns and Arborio rice cooked in white wine stock p202

Scallop, Prawn & Mint Salad With a light dressing of lime juice and rind and fresh parsley p205

Thai Prawn & Noodle Soup Amazing colour of coconut milk with red chillies and vermicelli p206

Mediterranean Fish Soup Fish and shellfish in a saffron and orange broth p208

Seafood Gumbo Classic Louisiana fish, prawn and okra stew served over rice p211

Loster with Basil Dressing With a dressing of sun-dried tomatoes, basil, walnut oil and sherry p213

Crab & Black Bean Sauce Stir-fried ginger, chillies, rice wine and fermented black beans p214

Crab Soufflé Folded into soft cheese, with Parmesan, parsley and anchovy essence p217

Cajun Crab Cakes White and brown crabmeat with onions and red pepper p218

Cioppino White fish fillets, scallops and prawns with tomatoes, white wine stock and herbs p220

Seafood Paté Fish fillets and prawn, with a luxurious touch from cognac or brandy p222

Taramasalata Create your own with bread, herbs, tarama and onion to discover the difference p223

Seafood Toasts Deep-fried golden prawn and ginger triangles, a popular fish appertizer p224

Cucumber with Mussels Cream cheese, cucumber and Tabasco sauce p227

Stuffed Mussels Filled with lemon, parsley and Dijon mustard and grilled p229

Mussels in Tomato Sauce Wine, tomatoes, lemon rind and capers to enliven p231

Herb & Garlic Mussels A butter of fresh parsley, dill and chives coloured under the grill p232

Indonesian Steamed Mussels Clams or mussels with a sweet and sour sauce p235

Oysters Rockefeller Pernod or pastis and Tabasco sauce for the tycoon touch p236

Oysters with Caviar Horseradish, sour cream and black caviar for an impressive effect p238

Angels on Horseback Classic and delightful rounds of bacon and oysters p241

Oysters in Beds Brioche shells and sour cream, excellent with tarragon salad p242

Kedgeree The ultimate breakfast, with haddock or salmon, rice and boiled eggs p245

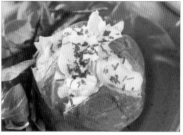

Haddock in Jacket Potatoes With sour cream, chives and parsley; make a great supper p246

Omlette Arnold Bennett Haddock, cream and Cheddar cheese, well done Arnie p249

Smoked Salmon Scramble With cream, lovely with toasted bagels or muffins p251

Smoked Salmon Quiches The smoked salmon in puff pastry can be garnished with caviar for special occasions p252

Introduction

The British adore seafood, and are eating more and more of it each year. Seafood evokes memories of shrimping, crabbing and watching fishermen return with their catches. It is these happy memories which contribute to many people's love of seafood. What other valuable food is available in such variety?

Nothing tastes quite like fresh seafood; it is naturally tender and will only toughen if overcooked. There is such a tremendous variety of seafood available that it makes sense to learn more about this crucial source of nutrients, and how it can best be incorporated into a diet which will please the whole family.

Fish is a wonderful food which is high in body building proteins and low in calories. White fish contains practically no fat, whilst oily fish varies in fat content from 0.5%–20% and contains the sort of fatty acids which doctors believe may actually assist in preventing coronary heart disease.

Fish also contains almost no carbohydrate and is an excellent source of vitamins. Oily fish is particularly high in the fat soluble vitamins A and D, thiamin and riboflavin.

With all these important benefits to boast of, it is obvious why more use should be made of this easy-to-obtain food which is both delicious and nutritious. Sadly, many people have misconceptions about fish and shellfish, believing it is difficult to prepare and cook. This is just not true, follow the instructions given in the following pages and the different methods of preparing and cooking will become surprisingly simple.

One of the most common complaints about fish is that it smells. A famous chef once said 'Fish should smell like the tide. Once they smell like fish, it's too late'. So make sure when you buy fish that it has a wonderful 'straight from the shore' aroma and is moist and fresh.

CHOOSING FISH

Fish can be classified in different ways – firstly according to the type of flesh:

White Fish has a distinctive white flesh and includes such favourites as cod, sole and sea bass.

Oily Fish has oil distributed through its flesh, giving it a grey or red tinge. This group includes trout, mackerel and sardines.

Shellfish is the group enclosed in a shell and is further classified into two groups – crustaceans usually have limbs and a shell, such as crabs and lobster, whilst molluscs, e.g. mussels, oysters etc. have a shell only.

Fish are also classified into groups determined by their shape:

Round Fish have a rounded body with eyes at either side of the head and always swim dorsal fin up. This is a very large group which includes a whole range of fish from freshwater salmon to sharks.

Flat Fish have both eyes on the top of their head; they swim on their sides, and are quick and easy to cook. This group includes skate and flounder.

BUYING FISH

When selecting fresh fish for the table it is important to choose the freshest fish possible. It is advantageous to buy a whole fish as it is very often cheaper than prepared cuts and is easier to judge for freshness. It should look moist and fresh, the eyes should be bright, the flesh firm, the gills red, the scales should sparkle and there should definitely be no unpleasant odour! Some fish have a natural slime which is easily removed by rinsing so don't be put off by it. If it is not possible or desirable to buy a whole fish, use the same guidelines when you select fish fillets or steaks. The flesh should look moist, bright, and white fish should be really white.

If possible, fish should be used on the day of purchase, but if it must be stored it should be cleaned, washed and kept in the refrigerator overnight in a sealed container. Shellfish should be bought alive, if possible, and used within 24 hours.

You will find a wide variety of fish and seafood at your local fishmonger, all of which you can buy ready prepared or whole. Cleaning and preparing fish is not at all difficult, just follow the step-by-step photographs and you will be surprised at how quickly you can have your fish ready for cooking.

Frozen Fish

Fresh fish is seasonal but frozen fish is, of course, available all year round. It is an excellent way to buy fish as only the best quality fish is frozen and it is frozen as soon as it is caught to preserve the freshness. Frozen fish is almost always prepared for cooking before freezing, making it particularly easy for the cook to handle.

White fish may be stored in a domestic freezer for up to four months, whereas oily fish, because of its high fat content, is best consumed within three months. Shellfish, particularly prawns, should be consumed within two months of being frozen. Homemade fish dishes also freeze well, but should also not be stored for longer than two months. For the best results defrost frozen fish overnight in the refrigerator.

Canned Fish

Canned fish is a wonderful store cupboard standby which keeps fresh more or less indefinitely and is therefore valuable for outdoor enthusiasts and the like, as well as for convenience meals when unexpected guests arrive. Oily fish, such as tuna and sardines, is particularly suitable for canning and can be used in a large number of recipes.

ABOVE: *Fish can be bought in a wide variety of shapes, sizes and cuts, providng a wealth of choice for the cook.*

Smoked Fish

Smoking is a method of preserving fish which results in its characteristic smoky flavour – kippers are probably one of the best known smoked fish available; however smoked mackerel is also widely available and is often served as a starter. Smoked salmon, which is always a favourite, is prepared by cleaning and filleting the fresh fish, then smoking the fillets in a cold smoker, often over apple chips and oak sawdust. The resulting smoked fish has a strong colour, translucent appearance and tastes wonderful!

NUTRITIONAL VALUE

Nutritionally speaking, fish is one of the most valuable foods available to man. It is an excellent source of protein, which is needed for the growth and repair of body cells. It is also low in carbohydrates and saturated fats. Oily fish is rich in the fat-soluble vitamins A and D and all fish is rich in thiamine, riboflavin, niacin, B6, B12 pantothenic acid and biotin.

Fish is also an excellent source of minerals, which are necessary for the body's growth and maintaining vital functions. Some of the smaller varieties of fish that can be eaten whole, bones and all, can also provide a useful amount of calcium.

Fish is also fairly low in calories, especially when compared with other valuable protein foods such as meat and cheese. The approximate calorie counts in the table below indicate just how useful fish is as part of a healthy diet:

FOOD	CALORIES
25g/1 oz of cod, steamed or poached in water	24
25g/1 oz of raw, ground beef	55
25g/1 oz of leg of pork	72
25g/1 oz of Cheddar cheese	102
25g/1 oz of tuna in brine, canned	32

PREPARING FISH AND SEAFOOD

How to Scale and Fin a Round Fish

• Holding the fish firmly by the tail, scrape towards the head of the fish with a scaler or the blunt side of a knife (see Fig. 1).

• Rinse the fish thoroughly under cold running water to remove any remaining scales and residue which may be clinging to the skin.

• Trim the dorsal fin with a pair of scissors. To remove the whole fin, snip through most of the fin in the direction of the head and then pull (see Fig. 2).

FIG. 1

FIG. 2

Cleaning a Round Fish

• Holding the body of the fish firmly cut the head off just behind the gills. The head can be saved for use in fish stock or soup, if wished.

• Cut down the underside to the tail and remove the innards, which should come out with ease (see Fig. 3).

FIG. 3

FIG. 4

FIG. 5

• Clean and remove any remaining residue and any blood by rinsing the fish thoroughly in cold running water.

Filleting a Round Fish

• Holding the fish firmly, cut along the backbone from just behind the head to the tail.

• Cut across the fish and slide the knife between the ribs and the flesh (see Fig. 4).

• Carefully lift the fillet away, taking care not to break up the flesh.

Skinning a Flat Fish

• Dip your fingers in salt to get a good grip on the fish, then hold the fish by its tail and make a cut across the skin just above the tail (see Fig. 5).

• Begin peeling the skin away from the cut. Pull the

skin over the head, turn the fish over and pull the skin off of the underside.

Filleting a Flat Fish

• After skinning the fish, if desired, cut down, but not through, the backbone starting from behind the head moving down towards the tail.

• Insert the knife under the flesh at the top of the fish and cut down between the flesh and the bones until the fillet lifts off. Repeat the process on the other side (see Fig. 6).

Skinning a Fillet

• Get a firm grip on the tail end of the fillet, then make a cut across the flesh and ease the fillet away from the skin with a sawing motion (see Fig. 7).

FIG. 6

FIG. 7

Opening Oysters

• Hold the oyster tightly in one hand, and with the other, insert the oyster knife into the hinge, twisting until the shell opens.

• Slide the blade under the oyster and cut through the connecting muscle to separate the oyster from its shell.

FIG. 9

FIG. 8

Preparing Mussels

• Scrub the mussels to remove any sand or barnacles

• De-beard the mussels by pulling the byssus which protrudes from the shell (see Fig. 8).

Removing Meat from Hard-Shell Crab

• Hold the crab firmly, twist the apron flap and gently pull, removing the intestinal vein which is attached to the apron (see Fig. 9).

• Holding the crab firmly with one hand, gently prise the shell off and put to one side for later use (Fig.10).

• Remove the gills or "dead men's fingers" and discard (see Fig. 11).

• Crack the crab in two and remove any meat left on the central body section

• Crack open the legs and extract the leg meat with a crab skewer.

• Scoop out the soft brown meat from the crab shell.

• If using the shell to serve the meat, break off the rough edges and cut to form a neat edge.

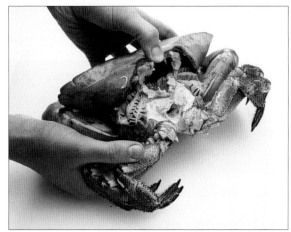

FIG. 10

FIG. 11

FIG. 12

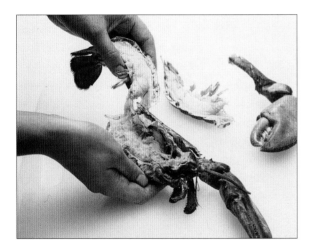

FIG. 13

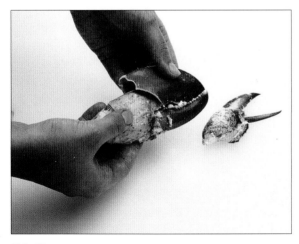

FIG. 14

Preparing Lobster

• Using a sharp knife, cut the lobster down the centre, beginning behind the head.

• Cut right through the lobster from head to tail to separate in two.

• Remove the tomalley (green liver) from the lobster (see Fig. 12).

• Holding the body of the lobster, break the tail section away from the body (see Fig. 13).

• Break the tail section apart and remove the meat.

• Cut the large part of the claw away from the bits which do not contain any meat. Crack the claws open to remove the meat (see Fig. 14).

• The easiest way to remove the meat from the claws is with your fingers. The meat from the shells should come out in one piece.

FIG. 15

Preparing Prawns

• Remove the legs of the prawn and break off the shell by bending both sides backwards.

• Cut down the back of the prawn, cutting deep enough just to expose the intestinal vein which should then be removed (see Fig.15).

FIG. 16

FIG. 17

FIG. 18

Preparing Squid

• Detach the tentacles and hard beak from the body of the squid by holding the tentacles and pulling gently (see Fig. 16).

• Remove the transparent quill and any remaining entrails by running your fingers along the body to the open end (see Fig. 17).

• Peel off the skin by pulling from the cut end to the tail (see Fig. 18). The squid is now ready for use.

COOKING METHODS

Fish and shellfish cook quickly and it is important to keep a close watch on its progress as it cooks. Overcooked fish becomes dry with a cotton-wool like texture. Shellfish becomes tough and rubbery. When cooked, the flesh of the fish loses its transparent quality and becomes opaque. The flesh of both fish and shellfish feels firmer when cooked, and the flakes of certain fish can often be felt through the skin. Certain shellfish, such as prawns and lobster, turn the classic pink-orange colour when done. Sometimes a curd-like white substance will appear on the surface of the fish. Although this is perfectly normal, too much of this white albumin can indicate that the fish has been overcooked.

Microwave Cooking

The microwave can be used for both defrosting and cooking fish. Timing is critical when microwaving fish and will differ according to the output of your particular model. Remember also that the more you put into a microwave, the longer it will take to cook as the energy has to be shared between the amount of food in the cabinet. Standing time should also be considered, as food continues to cook for a short period after being removed from the microwave and this must be allowed for when cooking fish. It is always better to undercook as you can pop the fish back into the oven for a minute or two after the standing time has ended. General rules for microwaving fish are as follows:

• Arrange the fish in a single layer in a shallow dish. Always cover during cooking, unless using a browning dish to achieve a crisp finish. Covering helps keep the fish moist, speeds up the cooking time and keeps the flavour in the fish.

• Always cook foods in non-metallic containers; this includes those which have a metal rim or trim.

• Whether your particular model has a turntable or not, always turn the fish over once during cooking.

• When cooking fish steaks, arrange them in a ring keeping thicker parts towards the outside of the dish.

• If the recipe calls for it, remember to stir as in a fish stew or soup – stirring, and turning where stirring is not advisable, are important parts of microwave cooking and help to ensure even cooking results.

• Always cook fish for the minimum advised cooking

time – it can always go back in the microwave after the standing time if necessary.

• Fish benefits by the addition of a little liquid – add water, stock or lemon juice.

• Do not add salt before microwaving as it tends to cause dryness.

Defrosting Fish

Frozen fish may be successfully defrosted using the defrost control on your microwave. Always lay the fish out in a single layer in a covered dish and turn over once half way through defrosting. Follow the chart in the manufacturer's manual supplied with your oven so that you have a guide as to timings. Allow a standing time between defrosting and cooking as the fish will continue to defrost during this time.

Fish can be cooked straight from frozen on 100% Full power in the microwave, although generally, it is easier to achieve perfect results if the fish is defrosted first. To cook straight through from frozen, simply double the cooking time given for cooking fresh fish, checking frequently and remembering to turn the fish during cooking and to allow a standing time at the end – 3–4 minutes standing is sufficient for most recipes.

Barbecuing

Fish and seafood cook quickly and easily, and is therefore one of the best foods to cook by this method. Remember that fish barbecues quickly, so always oil the grill rack and kebab sticks or fish grids and either marinate white fish or brush with oil before cooking. Add a little seasoning and some fresh herbs before cooking to impart a delicate flavour to the fish.

Choose firm fish that will not disintegrate during cooking and cut into thick fillets or chunks for kebabs or barbecue whole fish with the cleaned belly filled with herbs. Make 2 or 3 slashes in the skin of whole fish before cooking and turn 2 to 3 times. Small whole fish will benefit from being wrapped in foil parcels before grilling. They will take about 30 minutes, so

cook them arranged towards the edge of the barbecue, and add herbs such as thyme and rosemary, seasoning and a little lemon juice to the parcels before cooking.

For a delicious marinade, combine 240 ml/8 fl oz dry cider with 60ml/2 fl oz walnut or olive oil, 1 clove of crushed garlic, and 1 tablespoon mixed, crushed fresh herbs such as rosemary, thyme and marjoram. Add $1/4$ teaspoon of salt and a little finely ground black pepper. Mix well and pour over the fish. This amount of marinade will be sufficient for 6 people.

Braising

As fish cooks quickly it may seem slightly unusual to think of a fish casserole. However, it is a good, moist method of cooking some of the less expensive cuts of fish. By this method large chunks of fish are cooked on top of a selection of chopped root vegetables which have been stir-fried in a little melted butter until softened and starting to brown. Liquid in the form of stock, wine, cider or apple juice to just cover the fish is added with a little seasoning and some fresh herbs.

The pan is then covered with a lid and left over a gentle heat until the fish is tender. Serve the fish with accompanying vegetables and liquid – thicken the sauce after lifting the fish if desired, but if you serve chunks of fresh bread with the stew your family or guests can simply soak up the juices with the bread.

Baking

This is an ideal method for cooking whole fish and is also excellent for large fillets or steaks of fish. Fish is usually baked in an oven preheated to 180C–200C /350F–400C/Gas mk 4–6. Prepared whole fish is delicious cooked on its own, simply seasoned and stuffed with a few herbs-remember to slash the skin in a few places to ensure even cooking. Lay in a shallow dish or roasting tin and bake, uncovered. Small fish such as trout will be done when the eye becomes opaque and the dorsal fin can be pulled out easily. The firm flakes of the fish can be felt underneath the skin.

With larger fish, such as a whole salmon, remove the dorsal fin and peek inside the slot where it was removed to see if the fish is done to your liking. Fish fillets or steaks of fish can be baked and will benefit from the addition of a little liquid in the form of stock or wine and should be baked covered with a lid or foil. Be careful not to overcook the fish – test frequently and remove as soon as the flesh flakes easily.

Grilling

This quick method of cooking is a popular way of dealing with fish fillets, steaks or small whole fish. The fish should be seasoned and then brushed with a little oil. Position the grill rack at its lowest level and then line it with foil before arranging the fish onto the foil. The speed of cooking will vary according to the type of grill and how near the fish is to the heat. The fish will need turning once or twice during cooking and remember to test frequently to see if the fish is cooked.

Fish is best cooked under a medium heat which allows the heat to penetrate more evenly right through to the centre.

Deep-Fat Frying

This is a fast method of cooking small whole fish such as whitebait. It is also a useful method for cooking

small pieces of fish dipped in batter. It is important that the oil is clean and of sufficient depth to cover the food. If the oil is not heated to a sufficient temperature before the food is added, the resulting fish will be soggy, as the heat of the oil will not have immediately sealed the outside of the fish. However, if the oil is too hot, the outside of the food will burn before the inside has had time to cook. The ideal temperature is usually 180C/350F (to test place a cube of bread in the oil – it should brown in 40 seconds).

As oil cooks food very quickly, fish, because of its very delicate nature, needs to have a protective coating before it is exposed to the extreme temperature of the oil. The coating helps to stop the fish breaking up and also acts as a seal, locking in the flavour. Seasoned flour, batter or egg and breadcrumbs are all suitable coatings. Cook small quantities at a time so that the temperature of the oil is not reduced.

Shallow Frying

This is a quick method of cooking fairly small amounts of fillets, fish steaks and small whole fish such as herring and mackerel. The fish should be protected with some sort of coating – dipped in beaten egg and rolled in breadcrumbs is ideal or dipped in milk and then rolled in flour or oatmeal. The oil should come just under half way up the pan and be heated until a shimmery haze rises from the pan. Add the fish and quickly seal both sides then reduce the heat slightly and cook until crisp and golden, turning once or twice. Once the food is cooked it should be drained well on paper towels and served immediately.

Stir Frying

Stir frying is done in a large shallow frying pan, or ideally, in a wok. It is a useful method for cooking small pieces of fish or shellfish quickly.

LEFT: *Fish stock is quick and simple to prepare – head, skin and bones can be supplied by your fishmonger.*

Start by stir frying prepared vegetables, such as onions and peppers, in a little oil, then add the fish, which will cook in 30 seconds to 1 minute. Always remember to assemble and prepare the ingredients before the oil is heated. The vegetables should be cut into even-sized strips. The whole meal is cooked and served all from one pan and usually accompanied by rice. The food is simply cooked, by stirring continuously over a fairly high heat, using a slotted draining spoon. Soy sauce is often added before serving but there is a wide range of sauces, such as oyster sauce, which are very tasty.

Poaching

Poaching is cooking gently in a liquid such as wine, water, fish stock or milk. Heat the liquid first then add the fish – both whole fish, fillets and fish cutlets are excellent cooked by this method. Cook them in a single layer, allowing the liquid to come about $3/4$ of the way up the fish. Season and cover with a tightly-fitting lid and poach small fillets and cutlets for about 8 minutes; whole fish may take 15–20 minutes.

Check continually and remove when the flesh at the thickest part of the fish flakes easily. The liquid should be used to make an accompanying sauce or reserved and used for fish soup.

Steaming

Steaming is an easy method of cooking fish fillets which ensures the fish remains juicy as it is surrounded by moisture whilst cooking. The fillet should be rolled or folded, lightly seasoned and steamed for 10–15 minutes in a steamer, covered with a closely fitted lid, over simmering water. Steamed fish is full of flavour so it can be served it on its own with freshly cooked vegetables, accompanied by a light parsley or cheese sauce, if required. The fish can also be steamed over water containing herbs to give a subtle flavour.

There's very little that can go wrong when steaming fish, simply ensure that there is sufficient water in the pan and that it is maintained at simmering point throughout the cooking process. Also, make sure that you cover the fish with a tightly-fitted lid, so that the steam which actually cooks the fish is kept in.

FISH STOCK

A good basic fish stock can be simply made using the head, skin and bones of white fish. It is quicker to make than meat stock and makes a delicately flavoured base for all types of sauces. To prepare the stock, put the fish heads, bones and skins into a large saucepan, and add a bouquet garni with some seasoning. Cover the bones etc. with cold water and simmer gently for 20–30 minutes. Strain and use as required.

NOTE

Nutritional Information
All values are per portion or per serving.
If a recipe serves say 4–6, the lower number has been used for the calculations.
Milk is semi-skimmed unless otherwise specified in the recipe.
Added salt: When a recipe stipulates "salt and pepper to taste" none has been included in the calculation. The amount added will have a dramatic effect on the final sodium (salt) content of the dish. When a recipe states, for example, $1/4$ teaspoon salt, this has been included.
Range of quantities for an ingredient: When the amount of an ingredient is shown as, say 25–50 g, a median value has been used in the calculations.
Stock: It is assumed that any stock used contains 1 g salt per litre.
Additional/optional ingredients: When a recipe states "serve with", "garnish with" or "optional" these ingredients have not been included in the calculation of the nutritional values.

FLAT FISH DISHES

Brill with Cardamom

[SERVES 4]

4 brill fillets, about 175 g/6 oz
  each
250 ml/9 fl oz fish stock
salt and pepper, to taste
2 teaspoons cornflour
juice 1 large lemon
seeds from 4–5 cardamom pods,
  toasted and ground
2 egg yolks
45 g/1½ oz unsalted butter,
  diced
lemon wedges, for garnish
tomato, orange and spring
  onion salad, to serve

1 Preheat oven to 180C/350F/Gas mk 4. Fold the fillets in half, then place in a single layer in a heavy baking dish. Pour the stock over the fish, cover and cook in the oven for about 18 minutes, until almost cooked. Transfer to warm plates, season, cover and keep warm.

2 Meanwhile, in a bowl, mix together the cornflour, lemon juice, cardamom seeds and egg yolks. Stir a little fish cooking liquid into the cornflour mixture.

3 Pour the remainder into a non-stick saucepan, then stir in the cornflour mixture. Heat gently, stirring, until the sauce thickens. Remove from the heat and gradually stir in the butter. Season with salt and pepper. Pour the sauce around or over the fish, garnish with lemon wedges and serve with a tomato, orange and spring onion salad.

NUTRITIONAL INFORMATION	
Kcal	280
Protein	33g
Carbs	2g
Fat	16g
Salt	0.6g
Sodium	220mg

Steamed Brill with Vegetables

[SERVES 4]

2 leeks, cut into fine strips
2 courgettes, cut into fine strips
2 sticks celery, cut into fine strips
3 spring onions, thinly sliced
2 sprigs thyme
3 sprigs parsley
1 small sprig rosemary
salt and pepper, to taste
2 tablespoons lemon juice
4 brill fillets
2 tablespoons olive oil infused
  with 1 tablespoon chopped fresh
  thyme

1 Bring a saucepan of salted water to the boil, then add the leeks, courgettes, celery and spring onions.

2 Boil the vegetables for 1 minute, then drain and refresh under cold running water. Lay in the bottom of a steaming basket. Add the thyme, parsley and rosemary and sprinkle with salt and pepper.

3 Drizzle the lemon juice over the fillets, fold them over and place on top of the vegetables. Add water to the base of the steamer, or a saucepan, and bring to the boil. Place the steaming basket on top and steam for about 4 minutes. Discard the herbs, season the fish, drizzle over the oil and thyme mixture and serve with the vegetables.

NOTE: Garnish with fresh sprigs of herbs, if wished.

NUTRITIONAL INFORMATION	
Kcal	240
Protein	33g
Carbs	3g
Fat	11g
Salt	0.6g
Sodium	230mg

Sole with Mint & Cucumber

[SERVES 4]

1 cucumber, halved lengthways,
   seeded and cut into 5-cm/2-inch
   fingers
salt and white pepper
4 sole fillets, about 175–200 g/
   6–7 oz each, skinned
1 small shallot, finely chopped
175 ml/6 fl oz fish stock
115 ml/4 fl oz medium-bodied dry
   white wine

175 ml/6 fl oz crème fraîche or
   double cream, plus a squeeze of
   lemon juice
5 mint leaves, torn
25 g/1 oz unsalted butter, diced
mint leaves, for garnish
mangetout, to serve

1 Place the cucumber fingers in a colander, sprinkle with salt and leave to drain for 30 minutes. Rinse and dry with kitchen paper.

2 Fold the fillets in half, skinned side in, and place in a frying pan with the shallot. Add the stock and wine and heat to just on simmering point. Poach for about 4–5 minutes, then transfer the fish to a warm plate and cover to keep warm.

3 Add the cucumber to the pan, increase the heat and boil until the liquid is reduced by three quarters. Add the crème fraîche and boil until beginning to thicken. Add mint, salt and pepper and the juices collected on the plate with the fish. Simmer gently for 3 minutes. Remove the pan from the heat and gradually swirl in the butter. Spoon the sauce over the fish and serve garnished with mint leaves, accompanied by mangetout.

NUTRITIONAL INFORMATION	
Kcal	400
Protein	33g
Carbs	3g
Fat	27g
Salt	0.5g
Sodium	210mg

Sole with Chive Sauce

[SERVES 4]

115 g/4 oz firm cottage cheese, drained and sieved
grated rind and juice of 1 lemon
salt and pepper, to taste
90 g/3½ oz cooked peeled prawns, finely chopped
8 sole or plaice fillets, skinned
225 ml/8 fl oz fish stock
1 small shallot, finely chopped
1 tablespoon dry white vermouth
6 tablespoons dry white wine
175 ml/6 fl oz double cream or fromage frais or soft cheese
1½ tablespoons finely chopped fresh chives
cooked prawns and chopped fresh chives, for garnish
steamed broccoli, to serve

1 Preheat oven to 180C/350F/Gas mk 4. Oil a shallow, ovenproof baking dish. Beat together the cheese, lemon rind and juice and season with salt and pepper. Mix in the prawns.

2 Spread on the skinned side of the fish fillets and roll up neatly. Secure with wooden cocktail sticks. Place in a single layer in the prepared baking dish, pour in the stock to come halfway up the rolls and add the chopped shallot. Cover and cook for about 20 minutes. Transfer the to a warm plate and keep warm.

3 Meanwhile, in a small saucepan, boil the vermouth and wine until reduced by half. Add the stock and shallot and boil hard until reduced by three quarters. Stir in the cream, if using, and simmer to a light creamy consistency. If using fromage frais or soft cheese, stir in and heat without boiling. Quickly pour into a blender and mix until frothy. Add the chives and season. Pour some sauce over the fish and serve the rest in a warm jug. Garnish the rolls with prawns and chives and serve with broccoli.

NUTRITIONAL INFORMATION	
Kcal	540
Protein	64g
Carbs	3g
Fat	29g
Salt	2.2g
Sodium	850mg

Sole with Lettuce Filling

[SERVES 2–4]

salt and pepper, to taste
4 sole fillets
squeeze of lemon juice
1 tablespoon medium-bodied dry
   white wine
1 tablespoon finely chopped leek
   (white part only)

85 g/3 oz Iceberg lettuce, finely
   shredded
85 g/3 oz ricotta cheese, sieved
1 egg white
lemon wedges and chervil sprigs,
   for garnish
beans and spring onions, to serve

1 Season the sole and sprinkle with lemon juice, cover and set side. In a small saucepan, heat the wine. Add the leek and cook for 2 minutes, shaking the pan occasionally.

2 Add the lettuce, cover and cook until the lettuce has wilted. Uncover, increase the heat and heat until the excess water has been driven off. Tip the lettuce mixture into a blender or food processor and add the ricotta cheese. Mix until smooth and then season.

3 Whisk the egg white until stiff but not dry, then lightly fold in the lettuce mixture. Place a quarter of the lettuce mixture on one half of each sole fillet, then fold the other half lightly over the filling. Place the fillets in a steaming basket or large colander. Cover and place over a saucepan of boiling water and steam for 10–12 minutes, until the filling is just set. Leave for 1–2 minutes then, using a fish slice, carefully transfer to warmed plates. Garnish with lemon wedges and sprigs of chervil and serve with beans and spring onions.

NUTRITIONAL INFORMATION	
Kcal	400
Protein	68g
Carbs	2g
Fat	12g
Salt	1.3g
Sodium	500mg

Plaice with Prosciutto

[SERVES 4]

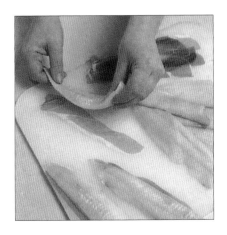

2$^1/_2$ large slices prosciutto ham
8 small plaice fillets
8 small sage leaves
2 tablespoons lemon juice, plus
   extra for seasoning
salt and pepper, to taste
1$^1/_2$ –2 tablespoons light olive oil
15 g/$^1/_2$ oz unsalted butter, diced
pasta, to serve (optional)
lemon rind shreds, for garnish

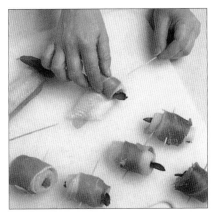

1 Cut the ham into 8 strips lengthways. Lay a plaice fillet on each piece of ham.

2 Put a sage leaf at one end of each fillet, season with lemon juice and pepper, then roll up and secure with a wooden cocktail stick.

3 In a non-stick frying pan, heat the oil, add the plaice rolls, seam side down, then cook until lightly browned all over. Transfer the fish rolls to a warm serving plate. Stir 2 tablespoons lemon juice into the pan and bring to the boil. Remove the pan from the heat and swirl in the butter. Season with salt and pepper, then pour over the rolls. Serve on a bed of pasta, if liked, garnished with lemon rind.

NUTRITIONAL INFORMATION	
Kcal	280
Protein	39g
Carbs	Trace
Fat	14g
Salt	1.1g
Sodium	440mg

Stuffed Sole

[SERVES 4]

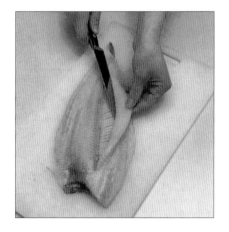

4 small sole, cleaned and dark skin
   removed
salt and pepper
1 tablespoon olive oil
1 small onion, finely chopped
2 cloves garlic, finely crushed
150 g/5 oz mixed mushrooms,
   such as oyster, shiitake and
   button, finely sliced
55 g/2 oz sun-dried tomatoes,
   thinly sliced

55 g/2 oz fresh brown
   breadcrumbs
1 tablespoon chopped fresh
   parsley
1 teaspoon chopped fresh
   marjoram
1–2 teaspoons anchovy paste or
   few drops Worcestershire sauce
mixed salad, to serve
lemon and lime wedges, for
   garnish

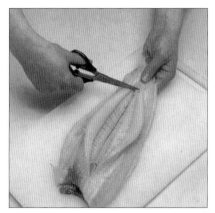

1 Preheat oven to 200C/400F/Gas mk 6. Butter a baking dish large enough to hold fish in a single layer. Place fish, skinned side up, tail towards you. Run point of filleting knife along line of backbone. Keeping blade firmly against rib bones, slice carefully lifting fillet as it is freed, until outer edge is almost reached – do not pierce through edge. Repeat with fillet on other side of the backbone.

2 Using scissors, cut through the top and tail end of backbone and snip the bones around the edges of the fish – do not pierce the underskin. Insert knife point under one end of backbone and lift up bone with the attached ribs and remove. Season inside and out with salt and pepper and place in the baking dish.

3 Heat the oil in a non-stick frying pan, add the onion and garlic and cook over a low heat until softened but not coloured. Add the mushrooms and tomatoes and cook over a higher heat to drive off most of the moisture. Stir in the breadcrumbs, herbs and anchovy paste and season to taste. Divide between the pockets in the fish, cover with foil and bake for 10–20 minutes, until flesh flakes. Serve with a mixed salad, garnished with lemon and lime wedges.

NUTRITIONAL INFORMATION	
Kcal	210
Protein	26g
Carbs	12g
Fat	7g
Salt	0.8g
Sodium	300mg

41

Fish & Pesto Parcels

[SERVES 2]

2 sheets filo pastry, 25 x 50 cm/
  10 x 20 inches, total weight
  about 55 g/2 oz
melted butter, for brushing
2 fish fillets (about 150 g/5 oz)
  each), such as salmon or
  turbot, skinned
55 g/2 oz cooked peeled
  prawns, finely chopped
55 g/2 oz button mushrooms,
  chopped
5 tablespoons fromage frais or
  low-fat soft cheese
2–3 teaspoons pesto sauce
salt and pepper, to taste
mixed salad, to serve

1 Preheat oven to 200C/400F/Gas mk 6. Butter a baking tray. Brush 1 sheet of pastry with butter, place the other sheet on top and brush with butter, then cut in half. Place a fish fillet in the centre of each pastry square. Top with prawns and mushrooms. Mix together the fromage frais and pesto sauce and season to taste.

2 Spoon a quarter of the pesto mixture onto each portion of mushrooms. Reserve the remaining mixture. Bring together 2 opposite edges of pastry and fold down over the fish. Fold the remaining edges over and tuck the ends under the fish. Brush with melted butter and place on the prepared baking tray.

NUTRITIONAL INFORMATION	
Kcal	550
Protein	40g
Carbs	18g
Fat	35g
Salt	1.8g
Sodium	720mg

3 Bake in the oven for 15 minutes, until browned. Using a fish slice, transfer to a warmed serving plate, split open the top of the pastry and spoon the remaining pesto into the opening. Serve with a mixed salad.

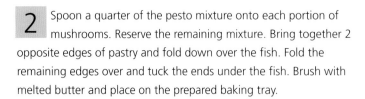

Turbot Parcels

[SERVES 4]

2 cloves garlic, unpeeled
2 large red peppers
2 teaspoons balsamic vinegar
1$^{1}/_{2}$ teaspoons olive oil
salt and pepper, to taste
8 spinach leaves, stalks removed
4 pieces turbot fillet, about
  165 g/5$^{1}/_{2}$ oz each
stir-fried mixed peppers, to
  serve

1 Preheat the grill. Wrap the garlic in foil and grill for 5–7 minutes to soften. Grill the peppers, turning, until evenly charred and blistered.

2 Leave the peppers until cool enough to handle, then remove the skins. Halve the peppers and remove the seeds and white membrane. Peel the garlic and purée with the peppers, vinegar and oil in a food processor or blender. Season with salt and pepper. Add the spinach leaves to a saucepan of boiling water and cook for 30 seconds. Drain, refresh under cold running water, then spread out on kitchen paper to dry.

3 Season the turbot, then wrap each piece in 2 spinach leaves. Place in a steamer basket or colander and cover. Bring the base of the steamer or a saucepan of water to the boil. Place the steamer basket or colander on top of the steamer base or saucepan and steam for 5–6 minutes. Heat the pepper sauce gently and serve it with the turbot parcels, accompanied by stir-fried mixed peppers.

NUTRITIONAL INFORMATION	
Kcal	180
Protein	29g
Carbs	4g
Fat	5g
Salt	0.4g
Sodium	170mg

Fish with a Mushroom Crust

[SERVES 4]

175 g/6 oz chestnut mushrooms,
  finely chopped
2 tablespoons lemon juice
2 tablespoons wholegrain mustard
2 firmly packed tablespoons fresh
  breadcrumbs
3 spring onions, finely chopped
1¼ tablespoons finely chopped
  fresh parsley

salt and pepper, to taste
4 turbot escalopes or fillets, about
  150 g/5 oz each
lemon slices and parsley sprigs,
  for garnish
courgette and tomato sauté, to
  serve

1 Preheat the grill. In a bowl, firmly mix together the mushrooms, lemon juice, mustard, breadcrumbs, spring onions, 1 tablespoon parsley and seasoning to taste.

2 Grill the turbot, skin-side up, for 2 minutes. Turn the fillets over, spread with the mushroom mixture and pat it down.

3 Grill the fish until the mushroom mixture has set and the fish flakes when tested with a knife. Sprinkle with the remaining chopped parsley. Garnish with lemon slices and sprigs of parsley and serve with a courgette and tomato sauté.

NUTRITIONAL INFORMATION	
Kcal	160
Protein	27g
Carbs	4g
Fat	4g
Salt	0.5g
Sodium	190mg

Turbot with Orange Sauce

[SERVES 2]

4 shallots
115 g/4 oz fennel, chopped
1 slim leek, sliced
small piece fresh ginger, peeled
  and sliced
350 g/12 oz turbot fillet
2 saffron threads, toasted and
  crushed

juice of 2 oranges
115 g/4 oz cold unsalted butter,
  diced
salt and pepper, to taste
orange slices and fennel or dill
  sprigs, for garnish
grilled fennel, to serve

1 Finely chop 2 shallots and set aside. Slice the remaining shallots and place in a steamer base or saucepan with the fennel, leek, ginger and 450 ml/16 fl oz water. Bring to the boil, then cover, remove from the heat and leave for 15 minutes. Transfer 115 ml/4 fl oz fennel liquid to a small saucepan and set it aside.

2 Using a slotted spoon, transfer the leek and fennel to the steamer basket. Bring the steamer base or saucepan back to the boil. Place the turbot in the steamer basket, cover and place over the pan. Steam for 10 minutes.

3 Meanwhile, add the chopped shallots to the fennel liquid in the small pan and boil until the liquid is reduced by two thirds. Add the saffron and orange juice and boil rapidly until reduced by two thirds. Lower the heat, then gradually beat in the butter, beating well after each addition. Season with salt and pepper. Transfer the fish to a warm serving plate, discarding the leek and fennel. Pour over the sauce and garnish with orange slices and fennel or dill sprigs. Serve with grilled fennel.

NUTRITIONAL INFORMATION	
Kcal	240
Protein	33g
Carbs	19g
Fat	4g
Salt	0.5g
Sodium	180mg

Halibut with Courgettes

[SERVES 4]

350 g/12 oz small courgettes,
  thinly sliced on the diagonal
4 halibut fillets, about 150–175 g/
  5–6 oz each
65 g/2¹/₂ oz unsalted butter
lemon rind shreds and juice of 1
  lemon
salt and pepper, to taste
4 sprigs parsley
lemon wedges and chervil sprigs,
  for garnish

1 Preheat the oven to 180C/350F/Gas mk 4. Generously butter 4 pieces of greaseproof paper large enough to loosely enclose each piece of fish.

2 Bring a saucepan of salted water to boil, add the courgettes and boil for 1 minute. Drain and refresh under cold running water. Pat dry. Make a bed of courgettes in the centre of each piece of paper. Place a piece of fish on each bed of courgettes.

3 Place a knob of butter on each fish, sprinkle with lemon rind shreds and juice, season with salt and pepper and top with a parsley sprig. Fold the paper over the fish and seal the edges tightly. Place the fish parcels on a baking tray and bake for about 15 minutes. Either serve the fish and courgettes in the parcels or transfer, with the cooking juices, to warm plates. Garnish with lemon wedges and chervil.

NUTRITIONAL INFORMATION	
Kcal	290
Protein	30g
Carbs	2g
Fat	18g
Salt	0.4g
Sodium	140mg

Halibut with Paprika

[SERVES 4]

4 teaspoons olive oil
175 g/6 oz shiitake mushrooms,
  stalks removed, sliced
salt and pepper, to taste
575 g/1¼ lb halibut fillets, cut
  into 1-cm/½-inch strips
1 onion, thinly sliced
1 large red pepper, seeded and
  thinly sliced

2 cloves garlic, finely chopped
2 teaspoons paprika
1 teaspoon plain flour
pinch of dried oregano, crumbled
115 ml/4 fl oz fish stock
115 ml/4 fl oz plain yogurt
rice, to serve
chopped fresh parsley, for garnish

1 In a non-stick frying pan, heat 2 teaspoons oil, add the mushrooms and cook gently for 5 minutes. Season with salt and pepper, cook for a further minute and then transfer to a plate.

2 Add the fish to the pan and sauté for 2–3 minutes, until just cooked. Transfer to a plate. Add the remaining oil to the pan, heat, then add the onion, pepper and garlic. Cook until softened. Stir in the paprika and cook for 1 minute.

3 Sprinkle the flour into the pan, then stir in with the oregano and stock. Cover and cook for 10 minutes. Transfer half of the pepper and onion mixture to a blender, add the yogurt and purée. Return to the pan with the mushrooms and any accumulated juices. Reheat gently without boiling. Add the fish and warm through. Serve on a bed of rice, garnished with parsley.

NUTRITIONAL INFORMATION	
Kcal	220
Protein	29g
Carbs	9g
Fat	8g
Salt	0.4g
Sodium	150mg

Yogurt-Topped Halibut

[SERVES 4]

2 tablespoons cumin seeds
2 tablespoons coriander seeds
2 large spring onions, chopped
2 cloves garlic, chopped
2 tablespoons chopped fresh mint
2 teaspoons dried dill
150 ml/5 fl oz plain yogurt
1 teaspoon paprika
salt and pepper, to taste
4 halibut steaks, about
    175 g/6 oz each
mint sprigs, for garnish
chicory, red onion and mint salad,
    to serve

1 Heat a small, heavy frying pan, add the cumin and coriander seeds and heat until fragrant.

2 Tip the seeds into a mortar or small bowl and crush with a pestle or the end of a rolling pan. Work in the spring onions, garlic, mint and dill, then stir in the yogurt and paprika. Season with salt and pepper.

3 Place the fish in a single layer in a shallow, heatproof dish. Spread the yogurt mixture over the top of each steak, cover and leave in a cool place for 2–3 hours. Preheat the grill. Grill the fish, basting occasionally, for about 10–15 minutes, until the fish is cooked and a crust has formed on the yogurt topping. Garnish with sprigs of mint and serve with a chicory, red onion and mint salad.

NUTRITIONAL INFORMATION	
Kcal	180
Protein	35g
Carbs	3g
Fat	7g
Salt	0.5g
Sodium	190mg

FIRM WHITE FISH DISHES

Chowder

[SERVES 4–6]

55 g/2 oz butter
1 large onion, chopped
2 large cloves garlic, chopped
6 sticks celery, chopped
450 g/1 lb potatoes, cut into
  small chunks
large pinch of cayenne pepper
600 ml/20 fl oz fish stock
600 ml/20 fl oz milk
1 bouquet garni
225 g/8 oz smoked haddock
  fillet
225 g/8 oz fresh haddock fillet
115 g/4 oz cooked peeled
  prawns
1/2 red pepper, seeded and diced
115 g/4 oz sweetcorn
salt and pepper, to taste
chopped fresh parsley or dill, for
  garnish

1 In a large saucepan, heat the butter, then add the onion, garlic and celery and cook until beginning to soften. Stir in the potatoes and cayenne pepper and cook for about 2 minutes.

2 Add the stock, milk and bouquet garni, bring to the boil, then cover and simmer for about 20 minutes, until the vegetables are almost tender. Meanwhile, skin both types of haddock and cut into bite-sized pieces. Add to the pan with the milk and simmer gently for 5–10 minutes, until the fish flakes easily.

3 Stir in the prawns, red pepper and sweetcorn and heat through. Season with salt and pepper and serve sprinkled with parsley.

NUTRITIONAL INFORMATION

Kcal	430
Protein	38g
Carbs	36g
Fat	16g
Salt	2.1g
Sodium	820mg

Haddock with Parsley Sauce

[SERVES 4]

4 haddock fillets, about 175 g/6 oz
  each
55 g/2 oz butter
3 tablespoons lemon juice
150 ml/5 fl oz fish stock
1 bay leaf
salt and pepper, to taste
4 teaspoons plain flour

150 ml/5 fl oz milk
4 tablespoons whipping cream
1 egg yolk
4 tablespoons chopped fresh
  parsley
green beans, lemon wedges and
  parsley sprigs, to serve

1 Place the fish in a frying pan, add half the butter, the lemon juice, stock and bay leaf. Season with salt and pepper. Heat slowly to simmering point, then lower the heat, cover and poach the fish for 10–15 minutes, depending on the thickness, until the flesh just begins to flake.

2 Meanwhile, melt the remaining butter in a saucepan, stir in the flour and then cook, stirring, for 1 minute. Gradually stir in the milk, then bring to the boil, stirring. Simmer for about 4 minutes, stirring frequently. Blend the cream into the egg yolk. Remove the pan from the heat and stir in the parsley and the egg mixture. Reheat gently, stirring, for a few minutes; do not allow to boil.

3 Transfer the fish to a warmed serving plate, cover and keep warm. Remove the sauce from the heat and stir in the fish cooking liquid. Discard the bay leaf, then pour into a warmed sauceboat to serve with the fish. Serve with green beans and lemon wedges, garnished with sprigs of parsley.

NUTRITIONAL INFORMATION	
Kcal	340
Protein	32g
Carbs	6g
Fat	20g
Salt	0.9g
Sodium	340mg

Haddock with Tomatoes

[SERVES 4]

4 tomatoes
4 tablespoons virgin olive oil, plus
  extra for brushing
1 shallot, finely chopped
1 small clove garlic, finely
  chopped
juice of 1 small lemon
1 teaspoon Dijon mustard

2 tablespoons chopped fresh
  chives
2 teaspoons chopped fresh parsley
salt and pepper, to taste
4 haddock fillets
chopped fresh chives and salad
  leaves, for garnish

1 Preheat the grill. Place the tomatoes under the grill, not too close to the heat, and grill until the entire skin is blistered and lightly charred, turning them frequently.

2 Remove the charred patches and any skin that comes off easily. Halve the tomatoes, remove the seeds and then dice the flesh. In a saucepan, heat 1 tablespoon oil. Add the shallot and garlic and cook until softened. Stir in the lemon juice and mustard, then whisk in the remaining oil. Add the tomatoes and herbs and season with salt and pepper. Keep the sauce warm over a low heat; do not allow to boil.

3 Heat a non-stick frying pan and brush generously with oil. Add the fish, skin side down, and cook for about 3 minutes, until the skin starts to crisp. Turn the fish over and cook for a further 2 minutes. Serve the fillets whole, placed on top of the sauce or slice into pieces and spoon the sauce over. Garnish with chopped chives and salad leaves.

NUTRITIONAL INFORMATION	
Kcal	290
Protein	30g
Carbs	4g
Fat	17g
Salt	0.6g
Sodium	220mg

Cod with Teriyaki Glaze

[SERVES 4]

2 tablespoons soy sauce
1 tablespoon rice wine or medium
sherry
1 tablespoon light brown soft
sugar
1 teaspoon grated peeled fresh
ginger
4 pieces cod fillet with skin
chervil sprigs, for garnish
stir-fried vegetables, to serve

1 Preheat the grill. In a small saucepan, gently heat together the soy sauce, rice wine or sherry, sugar and ginger for 2–3 minutes, until lightly syrupy. Leave to cool.

2 Grill the fish, skin-side down, for 3 minutes, then turn the fillets over and grill for 3-4 minutes, until the skin is crisp and the flesh almost cooked.

3 Turn the fish over again, brush the top liberally with sauce and return to the grill for 1 minute. Transfer to warm serving plates and pour over any remaining sauce. Garnish with sprigs of chervil and serve with stir-fried vegetables.

NUTRITIONAL INFORMATION	
Kcal	160
Protein	31g
Carbs	5g
Fat	1g
Salt	1.6g
Sodium	630mg

Roast Cod with Lentils

[SERVES 4]

3 tablespoons olive oil
3 shallots, finely chopped
2 cloves garlic, finely crushed
175 g/6 oz green or brown lentils
3¹/₂ teaspoons crushed coriander
  seeds
300 ml/10 fl oz fish stock
300 ml/10 fl oz dry white wine
2 tablespoons chopped fresh
  coriander

700 g/1¹/₂ lb cod fillet, cut into 4
  pieces
pinch of saffron threads, toasted
  and crushed
4 tomatoes, peeled, seeded and
  chopped
salt and pepper, to taste
coriander sprigs, for garnish

1 In a saucepan, heat 1¹/₂ tablespoons of oil, add the shallots and the garlic and cook gently until softened. Stir in the lentils and 3 teaspoons of the coriander seeds. Cook for 2 minutes, stirring, then add the stock and wine. Bring to the boil and simmer for 25–45 minutes, until the lentils are tender. Stir in the chopped coriander.

2 Meanwhile, preheat oven to 230C/450F/Gas mk 8. Heat 1 tablespoon oil in a non-stick roasting tin and fry the cod, skin side down, for 2 minutes. Transfer to the oven for 8 minutes.

3 Meanwhile, heat the remaining oil in a saucepan, add the remaining shallot, coriander seeds and saffron and cook gently until softened. Add the tomatoes, a little liquid from the lentils and season with salt and pepper. Cook gently for 5 minutes. Drain the lentils and season. Serve the cod garnished with sprigs of coriander and accompanied by the lentils and tomato relish, mixed together or separate as desired.

NUTRITIONAL INFORMATION	
Kcal	440
Protein	32g
Carbs	30g
Fat	13g
Salt	0.4g
Sodium	160mg

Fish Cakes

[SERVES 4]

450 g/1 lb potatoes, boiled
450 g/1 lb cooked mixed white
  and smoked fish, such as
  haddock or cod, flaked
25 g/1 oz butter, diced
3 tablespoons chopped fresh
  parsley
1 egg, separated
salt and pepper, to taste
1 egg, beaten
about 55 g/2 oz breadcrumbs
  made with stale bread
olive oil, for frying
lemon wedges, to serve
onion and avocado salad, to
  serve
dill sprigs, for garnish

1 In a saucepan, gently heat the potatoes for a few minutes, shaking the pan occasionally.

2 Remove the potatoes from the heat, mash, then beat in the fish, butter, parsley and egg yolk. Season with pepper. Transfer to a large bowl and mix well together. Chill if the mixture is soft.

3 Divide the fish mixture into 8 equal portions then, with floured hands, form each portion into a flat cake. In a bowl, beat the egg white with the whole egg. Spread the breadcrumbs on a plate. Dip each fish cake in the egg, then in the breadcrumbs. Heat a thin layer of oil in a frying pan and fry the fish cakes for about 3 minutes on each side, until crisp and golden. Drain on kitchen paper and serve hot with lemon wedges, onion and avocado salad, and garnished with sprigs of dill.

NUTRITIONAL INFORMATION	
Kcal	460
Protein	29g
Carbs	28g
Fat	26g
Salt	0.9g
Sodium	340mg

Fish Gratins

[SERVES 4]

1/2 teaspoon Dijon mustard
1 tablespoon lemon juice
1 tablespoon olive oil
pinch of freshly grated nutmeg
salt and pepper, to taste
4 cod or haddock steaks, about
 150 g/5 oz each
85 g/3 oz sharp Cheshire cheese,
 finely crumbled, or mature
 Cheddar cheese, thinly sliced
45 g/1 1/2 oz freshly grated
 Parmesan cheese
2 tablespoons fine fresh
 breadcrumbs
paprika, to serve
mangetout or pattypan squash,
 to serve

1 Preheat the grill. In a small bowl, whisk together the mustard and lemon juice using a fork, then gradually whisk in the oil. Add the nutmeg and season with salt and pepper.

2 Brush one side of the fish with the mustard mixture. Grill, coated side up, for 2 minutes. Turn and brush the other side with the mustard mixture and grill for a further 2 minutes.

3 Cover the fish with the crumbled or sliced cheese. Mix together the Parmesan cheese and breadcrumbs. Sprinkle evenly onto the fish, then season generously with pepper. Grill until the top is golden and bubbling. Lightly sprinkle with paprika and serve with mangetout or pattypan squash.

NUTRITIONAL INFORMATION	
Kcal	300
Protein	36g
Carbs	3g
Fat	15g
Salt	1.0g
Sodium	410mg

Goujons with Piquant Dip

[SERVES 4]

575 g/1¼ lb firm white fish such
  as hake, haddock or cod, skinned
salt and pepper, to taste
1 egg, beaten
55 g/2 oz fresh breadcrumbs
olive oil, for deep frying
lemon wedges and dill sprigs, for
  garnish

DIP:
3½ tablespoons gherkins
150 ml/5 fl oz low-calorie
  mayonnaise
6 tablespoons plain yogurt
2 tablespoons chopped dill
1 tablespoon capers, chopped if
  large
2 teaspoons Dijon mustard

1 To make the dip, finely chop the gherkins. In a bowl beat all the ingredients together, then cover and chill until needed.

2 Remove the bones from the fish, then cut the flesh into thin strips. Season the pieces with salt and pepper, dip in the egg then in breadcrumbs to coat evenly. Half-fill a deep fat fryer with oil and heat to 180C/350F.

3 Add the fish, in batches if necessary so the pan is not crowded, and fry until crisp and golden. Drain on kitchen paper and serve hot, garnished with lemon wedges and sprigs of dill and accompanied by the dip.

NUTRITIONAL INFORMATION	
Kcal	460
Protein	29g
Carbs	12g
Fat	33g
Salt	1.7g
Sodium	660mg

Hot Fish Loaf

[SERVES 4–6]

45 g/1¹/₂ oz butter
2 cloves garlic, crushed
3 tablespoons plain flour
425 ml/15 fl oz milk
575 g/1¹/₄ lb white fish fillets, such
  as hake or haddock, skinned and
  chopped
150 ml/5 fl oz double cream
2 teaspoons anchovy essence

3 eggs and 1 egg yolk
lemon juice, to taste
salt and cayenne pepper, to taste
115 g/4 oz cooked peeled prawns
2 tablespoons chopped fresh basil
basil sprigs, for garnish
wholemeal bread, to serve
  (optional)

1 Preheat oven to 150C/300F/Gas mk 2. Butter and line the base of a 1.6-litre/2³/₄-pint terrine or loaf tin. In a saucepan, melt the butter, then add the garlic and cook for 1 minute. Stir in the flour and cook, stirring, for 1 minute, then gradually stir in the milk. Bring to the boil, stirring, and simmer for about 3 minutes, stirring occasionally.

2 Pour into a blender, add the fish, cream, anchovy essence, eggs and egg yolk. Purée, then add lemon juice and season with salt and cayenne pepper.

3 Spoon half of the fish mixture into a terrine or loaf tin. Finely chop the prawns, then sprinkle them evenly over the fish with the chopped basil. Spoon the remaining fish over the top. Cover the terrine or loaf tin tightly with greaseproof paper, place in a roasting tin and pour in enough boiling water to come halfway up the sides. Bake for about 1³/₄ hours. Invert the terrine or tin onto a warm serving plate and tilt slightly to drain off the juice. Garnish with basil and serve with slices of wholemeal bread, if liked.

NUTRITIONAL INFORMATION	
Kcal	530
Protein	42g
Carbs	9g
Fat	37g
Salt	2.4g
Sodium	950mg

Whiting with Italian Sauce

[SERVES 4]

3 tablespoons olive oil
4 whiting fillets, about 175–200 g/
    6–7 oz each
2 onions, finely chopped
1–2 anchovy fillets, coarsely
    chopped
3 tablespoons chopped fresh
    parsley
175 ml/6 fl oz dry white wine
black pepper, to taste
parsley sprigs, for garnish
orange, cherry tomato and spring
    onion salad, to serve

1   Heat the oil in a frying pan. Add the whiting and fry for 2–3
    minutes on each side, until almost cooked. Transfer to kitchen
paper, cover and keep warm.

2   Add the onions to the pan and cook over a moderate heat until
    lightly coloured. Stir in the anchovies and parsley, stirring until
anchovies dissolve, then add the wine and boil until reduced by half.

3   Slip the fish into the pan, baste with the sauce, season with black
    pepper and heat for 2–3 minutes, basting occasionally. Serve
garnished with sprigs of parsley, accompanied by an orange, cherry
tomato and spring onion salad.

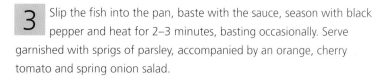

NUTRITIONAL INFORMATION	
Kcal	280
Protein	34g
Carbs	7g
Fat	12g
Salt	0.6g
Sodium	240mg

Sesame Coated Whiting

[SERVES 4]

1 tablespoon Dijon mustard
1 tablespoon tomato purée
1¹/₂ teaspoons finely chopped
   fresh tarragon
squeeze of lemon juice
black pepper, to taste
9 tablespoons sesame seeds
2 tablespoons plain flour

1 egg, lightly beaten
4 whiting fillets, about 150 g/5 oz
   each, skinned
olive oil, for brushing
red pepper, steamed courgette
   and leeks, to serve
tarragon sprigs and lemon
   wedges, thinly sliced for garnish

1 In a bowl, mix together the mustard, tomato purée, tarragon, lemon juice and pepper. In a separate bowl, combine the sesame seeds and flour and spread evenly on a large plate. Pour the egg onto another plate.

2 Spread the mustard mixture over both sides of each fish fillet, dip in the egg and then coat each fish evenly in the sesame seed and flour mixture. Refrigerate for 30 minutes.

3 Preheat the grill and oil the grill rack. Brush one side of each fillet lightly with oil, then grill for 2 minutes. Turn over, lightly brush the top side with oil and grill for a further 2 minutes. Using a fish slice, transfer the fish to a warm serving plate. Serve with red pepper, courgettes and leeks, garnished with sprigs of tarragon and lemon wedges.

NUTRITIONAL INFORMATION	
Kcal	490
Protein	29g
Carbs	6g
Fat	40g
Salt	0.4g
Sodium	150mg

Whiting with Spinach

[SERVES 4]

1 tablespoon light olive oil
1 small onion, finely chopped
175 g/6 oz button mushrooms,
    sliced
1 kg/2 lb spinach, stalks removed
25 g/1 oz butter
pinch of freshly grated nutmeg
salt and pepper, to taste
4 whiting fillets, skinned and
    halved lengthways
2 tablespoons freshly grated
    Parmesan cheese
dill sprigs and shavings of
    Parmesan cheese, for garnish

1 Preheat oven to 180C/350F/Gas mk 4. Butter a shallow baking dish. In a non-stick frying pan, heat the oil, add the onion and cook fairly slowly until softened but not browned.

2 Increase the heat, add the mushrooms and cook for 2–3 minutes. Add the spinach to the pan and heat, stirring frequently, until no surplus liquid is visible. Add the butter and season with nutmeg, salt and pepper.

3 Spread the spinach mixture in the baking dish. Season the whiting, then roll up with skinned side in and secure with wooden cocktail sticks. Arrange on top of the spinach mixture. Sprinkle with Parmesan cheese, cover and bake for about 20–25 minutes. Serve garnished with sprigs of dill and Parmesan cheese.

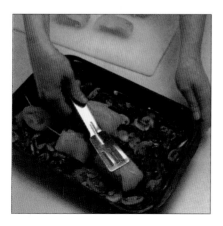

NUTRITIONAL INFORMATION	
Kcal	310
Protein	41g
Carbs	7g
Fat	14g
Salt	1.5g
Sodium	590mg

Monkfish in Coconut Cream

[SERVES 4]

seeds from 4–5 cardamom pods
3/4 teaspoon coriander seeds
1/2–3/4 teaspoon cumin seeds
generous 1-cm/1/2-inch piece fresh
    ginger, peeled and finely
    chopped
1 plump or 2 slim stalks lemon
    grass, crushed and finely
    chopped
salt and pepper, to taste
1 kg/2 lb monkfish tail

2 shallots
1 clove garlic
25 g/1 oz creamed coconut,
    chopped
150 ml/5 fl oz hot water
1 fresh red chilli, finely chopped
baby corn and baby courgettes, to
    serve
Chinese noodles, to serve
    (optional)
coriander sprigs, for garnish

1 Preheat oven to 180C/350F/Gas mk 4. Heat a heavy pan, add the cardamom, coriander and cumin seeds and heat until fragrant.

2 Tip into a mortar and crush finely with pestle. Crush in the ginger, lemon grass and season with pepper. Remove the fine skin and the bone from the monkfish, cut the flesh into 4 pieces and rub the spice mixture into them. Cover and leave for 30 minutes.

3 Finely chop the shallots and garlic together and place half in a shallow baking dish just large enough to hold the fish. Place the fish on top of the shallot mixture and scatter the remaining mixture over the top. Blend the coconut with the hot water until smooth, then pour over the fish. Season with salt and pepper, cover and bake for about 30 minutes. Toss together the chilli, baby corn and courgettes, then toss with the noodles (if using) and place in serving bowls. Place the fish on top and serve garnished with coriander.

NUTRITIONAL INFORMATION	
Kcal	210
Protein	38g
Carbs	2g
Fat	7g
Salt	0.4g
Sodium	170mg

Middle Eastern Monkfish

[SERVES 4]

2 cloves garlic
1 (6¹/4-cm/2¹/2-inch) piece fresh
  ginger, peeled
3 tablespoons olive oil
2¹/2 tablespoons tomato purée
1¹/2 teaspoons ground cinnamon
1 teaspoon caraway seeds,
  crushed
salt and pepper, to taste
1 kg/2 lb 4 oz monkfish tail
¹/2 Spanish onion, finely chopped
couscous and lemon wedges, to
  serve

1 Finely chop the garlic and ginger together. In a small bowl, stir the oil into the tomato purée, then stir in the ginger and garlic, cinnamon and caraway seeds. Season with salt and pepper.

2 Remove the fine skin from the monkfish, then spread with the spice mixture. Place the fish in a shallow dish, cover and leave in a cool place for 1–1¹/2 hours.

3 Preheat oven to 200C/400F/Gas mk 6. Cut a piece of foil large enough to enclose the fish. Make a bed of chopped onion on the foil and place the monkfish, and any remaining spice paste, on the onion. Fold the foil loosely over the fish and seal the edges tightly. Bake for 20–25 minutes. Open the foil, baste the fish and bake for a further 10–15 minutes. Serve on a bed of couscous, garnished with lemon wedges.

NUTRITIONAL INFORMATION	
Kcal	260
Protein	38g
Carbs	3g
Fat	11g
Salt	0.5g
Sodium	190mg

Chunky Fish Casserole

[SERVES 4]

100 g/3¹/₂ oz pasta shells
3 tablespoons olive oil
2 cloves garlic, finely crushed
85 g/3 oz button onions, halved
115 g/4 oz button mushrooms,
  halved
450 g/1 lb firm, white fish, such as
  cod or monkfish
225 g/8 oz trout fillets
3 tablespoons well-seasoned plain
  flour

225 g/8 oz broad beans
115 ml/4 fl oz dry white wine
300 ml/10 fl oz fish stock
1 large bouquet garni
grated rind and juice of 1 lemon
150 g/5 oz cooked peeled prawns
  or cooked shelled mussels or
  clams
chopped fresh herbs, for garnish

1 Preheat oven to 180C/350F/Gas mk 4. Cook the pasta in plenty of boiling salted water for three-quarters of time recommended on the packet. Drain and rinse under cold running water; set aside.

2 In a large frying pan, heat half of the oil, add the garlic, onions and mushrooms and cook for 3–4 minutes. Using a slotted spoon, transfer to a large, deep baking dish. Meanwhile, skin the fish and cut into 2¹/₂-cm/1-inch chunks, then toss in the seasoned flour.

3 Add the remaining oil to the pan, heat and then add the fish, in batches if necessary. Fry for 2–3 minutes, turning pieces carefully. Transfer to the baking dish and add the pasta and beans. Stir the wine, stock, bouquet garni and lemon rind and juice into the pan and bring to the boil. Simmer for a few minutes, then pour into the dish. Cover and cook in oven for about 30 minutes. Add the prawns, mussels or clams, cover again and cook for about 5 minutes. Garnish with chopped herbs.

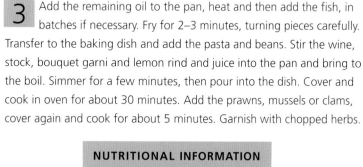

NUTRITIONAL INFORMATION	
Kcal	470
Protein	49g
Carbs	33g
Fat	15g
Salt	1.9g
Sodium	740mg

Monkfish on Ratatouille

[SERVES 4–6]

2 aubergines, halved lengthways
3 courgettes, sliced
salt and pepper, to taste
2 monkfish tails, total weight
  about 1.2 kg/1³/₄ lb
6 cloves garlic
5 tablespoons olive oil
1 Spanish onion, very thinly sliced

2 large red peppers, thinly sliced
4 large tomatoes, skinned, seeded
  and chopped
leaves from a few sprigs of thyme,
  marjoram and oregano
about 2 tablespoons each
  chopped parsley and torn basil

1 Cut the aubergines into 2¹/₂-cm/1-inch slices. Place in a colander with the courgette slices, sprinkle with salt and leave for 1 hour. Rinse well, then dry thoroughly with kitchen paper.

2 Meanwhile, remove the fine skin from the monkfish and cut slits in the flesh. Cut 3 garlic cloves into thin slivers and insert in slits. Season with salt and pepper and set aside. Chop the remaining garlic.

3 In a heavy flameproof casserole, heat 2 tablespoons oil, add the aubergine slices and sauté for a few minutes. Add another tablespoon of oil, plus the onion and garlic, and sauté for a few minutes. Add the peppers and cook for 1 minute, stirring occasionally. Add 2 more tablespoons of oil and the courgettes. Stir occasionally for a few minutes, then add the tomatoes, snip in the herb leaves and season lightly. Cover and cook very gently for 30–40 minutes, stirring occasionally, until fairly dry. Preheat oven to 200C/400F/Gas mk 6. Stir the parsley into the ratatouille and tip into a baking dish. Lay the monkfish on top and cook for 30–40 minutes, turning fish occasionally. Sprinkle with basil just before the end of the cooking time and serve.

NUTRITIONAL INFORMATION	
Kcal	410
Protein	43g
Carbs	12g
Fat	21g
Salt	0.5g
Sodium	180mg

Ceviche

[SERVES 4 AS A FIRST COURSE]

450 g/1 lb monkfish or halibut
  fillets, thinly sliced
1 fresh red chilli, seeded and
  thinly sliced
2 teaspoons coriander seeds,
  toasted and finely crushed
salt, to taste
juice of 4 limes
2¹/₂ tablespoons virgin olive oil

¹/₂ red onion, thinly sliced
1 beefsteak tomato, peeled,
  seeded and cut into thin strips
1 red pepper, seeded and chopped
1 tablespoon chopped fresh
  coriander
lime wedges, for garnish
lamb's lettuce and red chicory
  salad, to serve

1 Lay the fish in a shallow, non-metallic dish. Scatter over the chilli and coriander seeds and sprinkle with salt. Pour over the lime juice. Cover and leave at room temperature for 1 hour, or 2–4 hours in the refrigerator.

2 Drain off the juices from the fish and mix 2¹/₂ tablespoons with the oil; discard any remaining juices. Scatter the onion, tomato, pepper and chopped coriander over the fish.

3 Drizzle the oil mixture over the vegetables and fish. Serve garnished with lime wedges and accompanied by a lamb's lettuce and red chicory salad.

NUTRITIONAL INFORMATION	
Kcal	200
Protein	21g
Carbs	5g
Fat	12g
Salt	0.3g
Sodium	100mg

Grilled Fish with Coriander

[SERVES 4]

700 g/1¹/₂ lb grey mullet, bream or
  monkfish fillets
3 tablespoons olive oil
2 cloves garlic, crushed
1¹/₂ teaspoons ground toasted
  cumin seeds
1 teaspoon paprika
1 fresh green chilli, finely chopped

handful of coriander leaves, finely
  chopped
3 tablespoons lime juice
salt, to taste
rice, to serve
mint sprigs and lime wedges, for
  garnish

1 Preheat the grill. Place the fish in a shallow, non-metallic dish. In a small bowl, mix together the remaining ingredients, except the rice, mint and lime wedges.

2 Spoon the coriander mixture over the fish, cover and leave in a cool place for 3–4 hours, turning occasionally. Grill the fish for about 4 minutes on each side, basting with the coriander mixture occasionally, until the flesh flakes when tested with the point of a sharp knife.

3 Serve warm on a bed of rice, garnished with sprigs of mint and lime wedges.

NUTRITIONAL INFORMATION	
Kcal	220
Protein	30g
Carbs	Trace
Fat	11g
Salt	0.4g
Sodium	140mg

RICH FISH DISHES

Hake Baked with Potatoes

[SERVES 4]

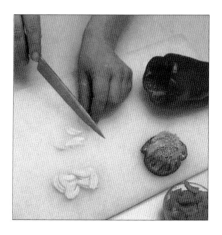

1 red pepper
450 g/1 lb new potatoes, very
  thinly sliced, rinsed and dried
1 onion, thinly sliced
1 large tomato, chopped
3 cloves garlic, slivered
4 tablespoons chopped fresh
  parsley
salt and pepper, to taste
225 ml/8 fl oz fish stock
  (optional)
700 g/1¹/₂ lb hake cutlets with
  skin, 2¹/₂ cm/1 inch thick
1 bay leaf
3 sprigs thyme
4 thin slices lemon
1 tablespoon olive oil
4 tablespoons dry sherry

1 Preheat oven to 190C/375F/Gas mk 5. Seed and chop the red pepper. Place half the potato slices in a large, lightly oiled baking dish. Scatter over the red pepper, onion, tomato, garlic and parsley. Season with salt and pepper and cover with the remaining potato. Pour over the stock, or 225 ml/8 fl oz water, cover and bake for 1 hour.

2 Increase the temperature to 220C/425F/Gas mk 7, uncover the dish and bake for about 7 minutes. Season the fish. Place the bay leaf and 3 sprigs of thyme on the potatoes.

3 Place the fish on top and nestle it into the potatoes. Lay the lemon slices on the fish, drizzle with oil and bake for 8 minutes, until the potatoes are crisp and brown. Pour the sherry over the fish and bake for another 2 minutes.

NUTRITIONAL INFORMATION

Kcal	290
Protein	34g
Carbs	25g
Fat	5g
Salt	0.4g
Sodium	150mg

Red Snapper with Crostini

[SERVES 2–4]

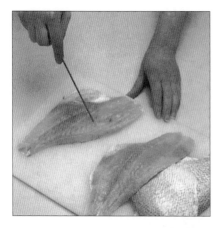

4 red snapper or red mullet fillets
4¹/₂ tablespoons olive oil
5 black peppercorns, coarsely
  crushed
1 orange, peeled and thinly sliced
juice of 1 lemon
1 small fennel bulb, quartered
salt and pepper, to taste

8 thin slices French bread
2 cloves garlic, cut in half
3–4 anchovy fillets
juice of ¹/₂ orange
1 tablespoon chopped fresh
  parsley
fennel sprigs and orange slices,
  for garnish

1 Prick the fish with a skewer, then place them in a single layer in a shallow, non-metallic dish.

2 Pour over 2¹/₂ tablespoons olive oil. Add the peppercorns and orange slices. Cover and leave to marinate in the bottom of the refrigerator, for 8 hours, turning occasionally. In a small saucepan of boiling water with the lemon juice added, cook the fennel until soft. Drain, then purée with ¹/₂ tablespoon olive oil in a food processor or blender. Season with salt and pepper and keep warm.

3 Rub the bread slices with the cut surfaces of garlic, then fry in the remaining olive oil. Keep warm. Drain the fish and reserve the marinade. In a frying pan, fry the fish in 1¹/₂ tablespoons marinade for about 3 minutes each side. Transfer to a warm plate, cover and keep warm. Add the anchovies to the pan, crushing them into the oil, then add the orange juice and parsley and heat through. Season with pepper, then pour it over the fish. Spread the fennel purée on the bread and serve with the fish. Garnish with sprigs of fennel and orange slices.

NUTRITIONAL INFORMATION	
Kcal	900
Protein	68g
Carbs	77g
Fat	38g
Salt	3.3g
Sodium	1320mg

Bream with Tarragon

[SERVES 4]

2 tablespoons white wine vinegar
1¹/2–2 teaspoons Dijon mustard
1 small shallot, finely chopped
1 clove garlic, finely crushed
115 ml/4 fl oz olive oil, plus extra
  for brushing
400 g/14 oz tomatoes, peeled,
  seeded and diced
1¹/2 tablespoons chopped fresh
  tarragon

2 tablespoons finely chopped
  fresh chives
salt and pepper, to taste
pinch of caster sugar (optional)
4 red bream or red mullet, about
  300 g/10 oz each, scaled
4 sprigs tarragon
tarragon sprigs and lime slices, for
  garnish

1 Whisk together the vinegar, mustard, shallot and garlic until the mixture is emulsified, then gradually whisk in the oil. Add the tomatoes, tarragon and chives and season with salt and pepper. Add a pinch of sugar, if wished, then leave to stand for 30–60 minutes.

2 Preheat the grill. With the point of a sharp knife, cut 2 slashes on each side of the fish. Season and push a tarragon sprig into each cavity and brush with oil. Grill for 10–11 minutes, turning and brushing with oil once.

3 Transfer to serving plates. Stir the tomato mixture, spoon some on to the fish and serve the remainder separately. Garnish with sprigs of tarragon and lime slices.

NUTRITIONAL INFORMATION	
Kcal	400
Protein	36g
Carbs	4g
Fat	27g
Salt	0.4g
Sodium	160mg

Sea Bass Under a Crust

[SERVES 2–3]

4–5 herb sprigs, such as tarragon,
  basil, fennel and parsley
5 crushed black peppercorns
1 kg/2 lb 4 oz sea bass, cleaned
  but not scaled, fins trimmed

2 kg/4$^{1}/_{2}$ lb coarse sea salt
tomato, basil, red onion and caper
  salad, to serve
lemon wedges and basil sprigs,
  for garnish

1 Preheat oven to 220C/425F/Gas mk 7. Place the herb sprigs and a few peppercorns in the cavity of the sea bass. Spread a layer of salt about 2$^{1}/_{2}$ cm/1 inch deep in a baking dish that the fish will fit into without too much space around it.

2 Place the fish on the salt, then pack salt around it until it is completely buried and there is a 2$^{1}/_{2}$ cm/1 inch layer on top. Bake the fish in the oven for about 25 minutes.

3 To serve, crack open the salt crust and remove the pieces carefully to expose the whole fish. Transfer to a large serving dish, remove the skin from the top of the fish and serve with a tomato, basil, red onion and caper salad, garnished with lemon wedges and sprigs of basil.

NOTE: The amount of salt and sodium have not been included in the nutrient calulation as the amount of salt remaining on the fish is extremely variable.

NUTRITIONAL INFORMATION	
Kcal	230
Protein	52g
Carbs	0g
Fat	2g
Salt	-
Sodium	-

Sea Bass with Garlic

[SERVES 4]

20 g/³/₄ oz unsalted butter
8 cloves garlic, with skin, lightly
  crushed
16 spring onions, cut into slices
4 sea bass fillets, about 200 g/
  7 oz each, with skin
salt and pepper, to taste
2 slices lean smoked bacon, cut
  into thin strips

1 sprig thyme
115 ml/4 fl oz fish stock
1 tablespoon chopped fresh
  parsley
parsley sprigs, for garnish
boiled new potatoes, to serve

1 Preheat oven to 200C/400F/Gas mk 6. In a heavy, shallow flameproof casserole, heat the butter, then add the garlic and spring onions and cook slowly until browned.

2 Season the skin side of the fish with salt and pepper, then place in the casserole, skin side down, with the bacon and thyme. Cook for about 2 minutes.

3 Turn the fish over and add the stock. Place the casserole in the oven and bake for 4–6 minutes. Stir in the parsley and add seasoning, if necessary. Garnish with sprigs of parsley and serve with new potatoes.

NUTRITIONAL INFORMATION	
Kcal	260
Protein	38g
Carbs	2g
Fat	11g
Salt	0.9g
Sodium	340mg

Bass with Ginger & Lime

[SERVES 6–8]

1 (4-cm/1¹/2-inch) piece fresh
  ginger, peeled and finely
  chopped
juice of 2 limes
2 shallots, finely chopped
4 tablespoons rice wine vinegar
225 ml/8 fl oz olive oil
2 tablespoons Chinese sesame oil

2 tablespoons soy sauce
salt and pepper, to taste
6–8 bass fillets, about 175 g/6 oz
  each, each 1 cm/¹/2 inch thick
leaves from 1 bunch of coriander
toasted sesame seeds, for garnish
stir-fried baby corn and sun-dried
  tomatoes, to serve

1 Preheat the grill. In a bowl, mix together the ginger, lime juice, shallots, rice wine vinegar, olive oil, sesame oil and soy sauce. Season with salt and pepper.

2 Brush the fish lightly with the ginger and lime mixture, then grill under a high heat for 2–3 minutes on each side.

3 Before serving, reserve a few coriander leaves for garnish, chop the remainder and mix into the remaining ginger and lime mixture. Place the fish on serving plates and spoon over the ginger and lime mixture. Sprinkle with sesame seeds and garnish with the reserved coriander. Serve with stir-fried baby corn and sun-dried tomatoes.

NUTRITIONAL INFORMATION	
Kcal	470
Protein	31g
Carbs	2g
Fat	37g
Salt	1.1g
Sodium	430mg

Spiced Bass

[SERVES 4]

4 bass steaks, about 150–175 g/
5–6 oz each
courgette and spring onion
salad, to serve
lemon rind and coriander
sprigs, for garnish

MARINADE:
1 cm/½ inch piece fresh ginger,
peeled
1 clove garlic
2 spring onions, sliced
1 tablespoon lime juice
1 tablespoon sesame oil
2 tablespoons grapeseed oil
½ teaspoon Chinese five spice
powder
2 tablespoons sake or dry
sherry

1 To make the marinade, in a blender mix the ginger, garlic, spring onions and lime juice to a paste. With the motor running, slowly pour in the oils, then add the five spice powder and sake or sherry.

2 Place the bass in a single layer in a non-metallic dish, pour over the marinade, cover and leave in a cool place for 1 hour. Preheat the grill. Remove the fish from the marinade and grill for about 4 minutes on each side, brushing with marinade when the fish is turned.

3 Serve with a courgette and spring onion salad, garnished with lemon rind and sprigs of coriander.

NUTRITIONAL INFORMATION	
Kcal	220
Protein	28g
Carbs	Trace
Fat	11g
Salt	0.3g
Sodium	130mg

Trout with Tomato Sauce

[SERVES 3–4]

65 g/2½ oz sun-dried tomatoes
2 teaspoons capers
8 basil leaves
leaves from 2 small sprigs
   rosemary
leaves from 2 sprigs oregano
pepper and salt, to taste
55 g/2 oz butter, plus extra for
   brushing
6–8 trout fillets
mangetout, blanched (to serve)
basil sprigs, for garnish

1 Roughly chop the sun-dried tomatoes, capers, and herbs to make a salsa.

2 Add to a bowl and season with pepper and just a little salt. Cover and chill until required.

3 Preheat the grill. Brush the trout with butter, season with pepper, then grill for 3–4 minutes on each side. Transfer the fish to warm plates, season with salt and spoon the salsa over the fish. Serve with blanched mangetout and garnished with sprigs of basil.

NUTRITIONAL INFORMATION	
Kcal	370
Protein	57g
Carbs	5g
Fat	14g
Salt	0.6g
Sodium	260mg

Trout with Hazelnuts

[SERVES 4]

115 g/4 oz hazelnuts in their shells
65 g/2½ oz butter
4 trout, about 300 g/10 oz each
salt and pepper, to taste
2 tablespoons lemon juice
1 tablespoon chopped fresh
    parsley
lemon wedges and parsley sprigs,
    for garnish
mixed leaf salad, to serve

1 Preheat the grill. Shell the hazelnuts, then spread in a single layer in the grill pan. Heat under the grill, stirring frequently, until the skins split. Tip the nuts onto a tea towel and rub to remove the skins. Roughly chop the nuts.

2 In a large frying pan, heat 55 g/2 oz butter. Season the trout inside and out with salt and pepper, then add 2 trout to the pan and fry for 12–15 minutes, turning once, until brown and cooked. Drain the fish on kitchen paper, then transfer to a warm serving plate and keep warm while frying remaining fish in the same way.

3 Wipe the pan with kitchen paper, add the remaining butter, then fry the chopped nuts until browned. Stir the lemon juice and chopped parsley into the pan, then quickly pour thr mixture over the fish. Garnish with lemon wedges and sprigs of parsley and serve with a mixed leaf salad.

NUTRITIONAL INFORMATION	
Kcal	430
Protein	47g
Carbs	1g
Fat	26g
Salt	0.8g
Sodium	300mg

Trout with Parma Ham

[SERVES 4]

4 trout, about 300 g/10 oz each
black pepper, to taste
1 lemon, quartered
4 sprigs basil or tarragon
4 slices Parma or prosciutto ham
lemon wedges, for garnish
cherry tomato, mangetout, chicory
  and lamb's lettuce salad, to serve

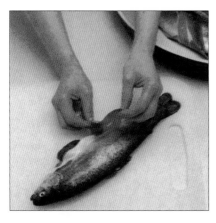

1 Preheat oven to 200C/400F/Gas mk 6. Season the trout with pepper and a squeeze of lemon juice. Place a sprig of basil or tarragon inside each fish.

2 Wrap a slice of ham around each fish and season with pepper. Place the fish in a large, shallow baking dish with the loose ends of ham underneath.

3 Bake the fish for 15–20 minutes, until cooked through and the flesh flakes when tested. Garnish with lemon wedges and serve with a cherry tomato, mangetout, chicory and lamb's lettuce salad.

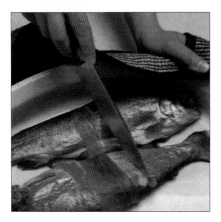

NUTRITIONAL INFORMATION	
Kcal	300
Protein	51g
Carbs	Trace
Fat	11g
Salt	1.0g
Sodium	430mg

Tandoori Trout

[SERVES 2]

seeds from 6 cardamom pods
2 teaspoons cumin seeds
4 tablespoons plain yogurt,
  preferably Greek style
1 large clove garlic, chopped
2 tablespoons lime juice
2¹/₂-cm/1-inch piece fresh ginger,
  peeled and chopped
1 teaspoon garam masala
pinch of ground turmeric

¹/₄ teaspoon cayenne pepper
salt, to taste
1 teaspoon red food colouring
  (optional)
2 trout, about 300 g/10 oz each
olive oil, for brushing
rice with chillies, to serve
tomato and onion salad, to serve
lemon and lime slices and
  coriander sprigs, for garnish

1 Remove the seeds from the cardamom pods. Heat a small heavy pan, add the cardamom and cumin seeds and heat until fragrant.

2 Tip into a mortar or small bowl and crush with a pestle or the end of a rolling pin. Place the yogurt, garlic, lime juice, ginger, all of the spices, cayenne pepper and salt into a blender and mix to a paste. Add the food colouring, if using.

3 With the point of a sharp knife, make 3 deep slashes in each side of the trout. Spread the spice mixture over the trout, working it into the slashes. Place in a shallow, non-metallic dish, cover and leave to marinate in the refrigerator for 4 hours. Preheat the grill. Brush the grill rack with oil. Sprinkle a little oil over the fish and grill for about 7 minutes on each side. Serve with the rice and a tomato and onion salad, garnished with lemon and lime slices and sprigs of coriander.

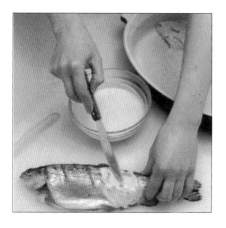

NUTRITIONAL INFORMATION	
Kcal	330
Protein	49g
Carbs	2g
Fat	16g
Salt	0.5g
Sodium	210mg

Trout & Artichoke Frittata

[SERVES 4]

1 medium or 2 small artichokes	2 tablespoons chopped fresh
45 g/1½ oz unsalted butter	parsley
6 eggs	salt and pepper, to taste
200 g/7 oz cooked trout fillet,	mixed leaf salad, to serve
flaked	

1 Snap off the artichoke stems, then bend the outer leaves backwards to remove them. Continue until the pale inner cone is reached. Cut off the tough top part of the cone and remove the hairy inner choke. Trim the artichoke and then quarter. Cut each quarter into 4 or 6 pieces.

2 In a 30-cm/12-inch frying pan, heat the butter and add the artichoke. Sauté for 2–3 minutes, then add a little water, cover and simmer until tender. Boil hard, uncovered, to evaporate off all of the water. Using a fork, lightly beat the eggs with the flaked trout, chopped parsley, salt and pepper until the yolks and whites are blended.

3 Pour the eggs into the pan and reduce the heat to very low. Cook very gently for about 15 minutes, until the bulk is almost set and the top is still creamy and moist. Meanwhile, preheat the grill. Place the pan under the grill for 30–60 seconds, until the frittata is just set. Loosen the edges with a spatula, then slide onto a warm plate. Serve in wedges with a mixed leaf salad.

NUTRITIONAL INFORMATION	
Kcal	290
Protein	25g
Carbs	1g
Fat	21g
Salt	0.5g
Sodium	190mg

Mixed Fish Pot

[SERVES 4]

1 red mullet, red snapper, bream
  or trout, about 350 g/12 oz
175 g/6 oz piece sea bass
350 g/12 oz monkfish fillet
1/2 bay leaf
11/2 tablespoons olive oil
115 g/4 oz fennel bulb
225 g/8 oz small carrots
115 g/4 oz onion, thinly sliced

1 small clove garlic, finely crushed
pinch of saffron threads, toasted
  and crushed
150 ml/5 fl oz dry white wine
5 tablespoons single cream
salt and pepper, to taste
1/2 bunch spring onions, cut
  diagonally into thin strips
dill sprigs, for garnish

1   Thickly slice the mullet, snapper, bream or trout and reserve. Place
    the head and tail in a small saucepan. Remove the skin and bones
from the bass and add them to the pan. Trim the fine skin from the
monkfish and add the skin to the pan with the bay leaf and 150 ml/5 fl
oz water. Simmer for 20 minutes, then strain and reserve the stock.

2   Thickly slice the raw bass and monkfish. In a flameproof
    casserole, heat the oil. Cut the fennel and carrots into thin strips
and add to the casserole with the onion, garlic and saffron. Cook for
3–4 minutes. Add 4 tablespoons wine and boil until most of the liquid
has evaporated. Add the remaining wine and boil until reduced by half.

3   Stir in the reserved stock, 2$\frac{1}{2}$ tablespoons cream and monkfish
    and season with salt and pepper. Cover and cook very gently for
10 minutes. Add the mullet and bass, cover and cook for a further 10
minutes or until fish is just cooked. Gently stir in the remaining cream
and scatter the spring onions over the top. Serve garnished with dill.

NUTRITIONAL INFORMATION	
Kcal	290
Protein	36g
Carbs	8g
Fat	11g
Salt	0.5g
Sodium	190mg

Salmon with Avocado Salsa

[SERVES 4]

4 salmon fillets with skin, about
175 g/6 oz each
2¹/2 tablespoons olive oil
sea salt and pepper, to taste
lime wedges and coriander leaves,
for garnish

SALSA:
1 ripe but firm avocado
2 large ripe tomatoes, peeled,
seeded and finely chopped
¹/2 small red onion, finely chopped
¹/2–1 fresh red chilli, seeded and
thinly sliced
1 clove garlic, finely chopped
2 tablespoons lime juice
2 tablespoons chopped fresh
coriander
salt and pepper, to taste

1 To make the salsa, halve the avocado, discard the stone, quarter each half and remove the skin.

2 Dice the avocado flesh and mix with the remaining salsa ingredients. Cover and chill in the refrigerator for about 1 hour.

3 Meanwhile, dry the fish well, then brush the skin with some of the olive oil. In a heavy frying pan, heat the remaining oil until hot. Add the salmon, skin side down, and cook for 10–15 minutes, depending on the thickness of the fillets, until the skin is quite crisp, the sides are opaque and the top is slightly soft as it should be rare. To serve, season with sea salt and pepper, garnish with lime wedges and coriander leaves and serve with the salsa.

NUTRITIONAL INFORMATION	
Kcal	480
Protein	34g
Carbs	4g
Fat	37g
Salt	0.5g
Sodium	180mg

Salmon with Herb Sauce

[SERVES 6]

1/2 onion, chopped
1 carrot, chopped
1 stick celery, chopped
1 lemon, sliced
1 (1.6-kg/3¹/2-lb) salmon
bouquet garni of 2 bay leaves and
   sprig each rosemary, sage and
   parsley
175 ml/6 fl oz dry white wine
salt and pepper, to taste
bunch of watercress, roughly
   chopped

3 tablespoons chopped fresh
   parsley
2 tablespoons chopped fresh
   chervil
1 tablespoon chopped fresh dill
225 g/8 oz mayonnaise
cucumber, peeled and sliced, for
   garnish
watercress and herb sprigs, for
   garnish

1 Preheat oven to 220C/425F/Gas mk 7. Place a large piece of foil on a large baking tray. Make a bed of vegetables on the foil and lay half of the lemon slices over them.

2 Place the salmon on top and add the bouquet garni and remaining lemon slices. Fold up the foil, pour in the wine, season with pepper, then seal the edges of the foil tightly. Bake for 30–40 minutes. Leave to cool completely in the foil. Strain the cooking liquid, then boil it until reduced to about 85 ml/3 fl oz.

3 Add the watercress and herbs and boil until softened. Tip into a blender, add the mayonnaise and purée. Thin with a little reserved fish cooking liquid, if necessary. Season with salt and pepper and refrigerate. Lift the fish onto a rack. Carefully remove the skin, fins and fatty line that runs along spine. Transfer to a large serving plate, garnish with cucumber, watercress and herb sprigs. Serve with the sauce.

NUTRITIONAL INFORMATION	
Kcal	710
Protein	45g
Carbs	1g
Fat	58g
Salt	0.8g
Sodium	330mg

Salmon & Avocado Mousse

[SERVES 4–6]

1 recipe Salmon Mousse (page 125), omitting cucumber
2 tablespoons gelatine
240 ml/8 fl oz cold water
2 avocados, halved and pitted
2 tablespoons lemon juice
2 teaspoons salt
1 tablespoon whipping cream
lettuce leaves and lime or lemon slices, to serve
melba toast, to serve (optional)

1 Prepare the Salmon Mousse and pour into a 750-ml/24-fl oz tin lined with cling film. The mousse should come two-thirds of the way up the side of the tin. Chill until beginning to set around the edges. For the avocado mousse, soften the gelatine in cold water in a saucepan. Warm over low heat, stirring until dissolved. Set aside.

2 Scoop the avocado flesh into a food processor, add lemon juice, salt and gelatine. Process. Add cream and blend. Put into a large piping bag with a plain tube. Hold the nozzle of the piping bag below the surface of the Salmon Mousse and pipe in the avocado mixture, at the same time running the pipe along to the end of the tin.

3 Chill the mousse until set. The mousse is easily removed from the tin by lifting the cling film. Serve slices on lettuce leaves. Serve with melba toast, if desired.

NUTRITIONAL INFORMATION	
Kcal	420
Protein	27g
Carbs	5g
Fat	33g
Salt	1.4g
Sodium	550mg

Salmon Stir-Fry

[SERVES 4]

450 g/1 lb medium slim asparagus,
  trimmed
2 tablespoons groundnut oil
300 g/10 oz salmon, skinned,
  boned and cut into thin
  2¹/2-cm/1-inch long strips
squeeze of lemon juice
1 tablespoon light soy sauce
2 teaspoons sesame oil
salt and black pepper, to taste
lightly toasted sesame seeds, for
  garnish
Chinese egg noodles, to serve

1 Slice the asparagus diagonally into 1-cm/¹/2-inch pieces. Bring a saucepan of salted water to the boil, add the asparagus and cook for 1¹/2 minutes. Drain and rinse.

2 In a preheated wok or large frying pan, heat the groundnut oil, add the asparagus and stir-fry for 1¹/2 minutes.

3 Add the salmon, lemon juice, soy sauce and sesame oil to the pan and stir-fry for 2 minutes. Add a little salt and black pepper. Serve immediately sprinkled with sesame seeds and accompanied by Chinese egg noodles.

NUTRITIONAL INFORMATION	
Kcal	270
Protein	18g
Carbs	3g
Fat	20g
Salt	0.8g
Sodium	300mg

Salmon Canapés

[MAKES 8]

225 g/8 oz canned red salmon
1/2 teaspoon paprika
freshly ground black pepper, to
   taste
1 tablespoon cream
2 slices pumpernickel (black) bread
25 g/1 oz butter
1 avocado
juice of 1 lemon
red caviar, for garnish (optional)

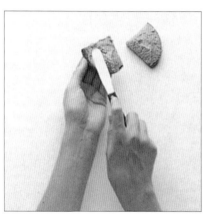

1 Drain the salmon, remove any bones and beat well with the paprika.

2 Flavour the salmon with a good grinding of pepper. Gradually beat in the cream. Cut each slice of bread into 4 triangles. Spread with butter. Pile the salmon mixture on to each piece of bread, smoothing with a knife.

3 Halve the avocado, remove the stone and peel. Cut the flesh into slices, then again into smaller pieces. Place a piece of avocado on each salmon mound and squeeze the lemon juice over. Garnish with red caviar, if liked.

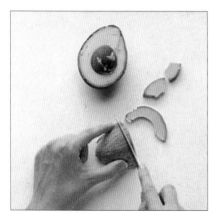

NUTRITIONAL INFORMATION	
Kcal	130
Protein	6g
Carbs	3g
Fat	10g
Salt	0.5g
Sodium	200mg

Chinese Salad with Salmon

[SERVES 4]

350 g/12 oz Chinese noodles
1 tablespoon salted black beans,
  coarsely chopped
85 g/3 oz beansprouts
1 tablespoon groundnut oil
450 g/1 lb salmon fillets, cut into
  2¹/₂-cm/1-inch cubes
2 teaspoons peeled grated fresh
  ginger

2 tablespoons rice wine or
  medium sherry
2 teaspoons sesame oil
85 g/3 oz watercress leaves and
  fine stalks
¹/₂ red pepper, seeded and
  chopped

1 Cook the noodles according to the directions on the packet, drain and rinse well with cold water. Drain again, then place in a serving bowl, cover and refrigerate while preparing remaining ingredients. Soak the black beans in 1–2 tablespoons hot water. Bring a pan of water to the boil, add the beansprouts and boil for 1 minute. Drain, rinse under cold running water, then set aside.

2 Heat the groundnut oil in a frying pan, add the salmon, in batches if necessary, and fry until just cooked and pale gold. Remove with a slotted spoon or spatula and drain on kitchen paper.

3 Stir the ginger, rice wine or sherry, sesame oil and half the watercress into a pan. Boil for a few seconds, then add the black beans and remove from the heat. Add the beansprouts, pepper and salmon to the noodles, pour over the warm dressing and garnish with the remaining watercress.

NUTRITIONAL INFORMATION	
Kcal	620
Protein	32g
Carbs	68g
Fat	25g
Salt	0.4g
Sodium	150mg

Salmon Mousse

[SERVES 4–6]

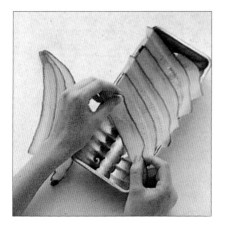

**1 cucumber (use a long one with
few seeds)**
**1 (400-g/14-oz) can red salmon,
drained**
1 tablespoon gelatine
125 ml /4 fl oz boiling water
1/2 teaspoon dry mustard
2 tablespoons white wine vinegar
1 teaspoon paprika
250 ml/9 fl oz single cream
**thin crispbreads or biscuits, to
serve (optional)**
lime slices, to serve

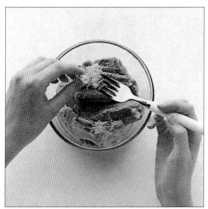

1 Trim the cucumber ends and cut lengthways into thin slices using a mandolin or cutter. Line a long narrow 500-ml/16-fl oz loaf tin with the slices.

2 Mash the salmon with a fork and remove any bones. Put the salmon flesh into a food processor and mix well. Dissolve the gelatine in the boiling water. Allow to cool but not set and pour over the salmon.

3 Add the mustard, vinegar and paprika and blend well together until smooth. Add the cream and blend until just mixed. Pour into the lined tin and chill until set. Turn out of the tin, cut into slices and serve on thin crispbreads or biscuits (if liked) with lime slices.

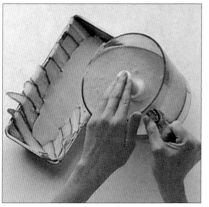

NUTRITIONAL INFORMATION	
Kcal	280
Protein	23g
Carbs	4g
Fat	20g
Salt	1.5g
Sodium	580mg

Salmon Puffs

[MAKES ABOUT 25]

125 g/4 oz plain flour
125 ml/4 fl oz water
1/2 teaspoon salt
55 g/2 oz butter
25 g/1 oz Cheddar cheese, grated
2 eggs

1 (200-g/7-oz) can red salmon
2 tablespoons mayonnaise
1 tablespoon pimento-stuffed
  green olives
red or black caviar (optional)

1 Preheat oven to 200C/400F/Gas mk 6. Grease 2 baking sheets. Sift the flour. In a saucepan, heat the water, salt and butter until the butter is melted, stirring constantly. Bring the mixture to a full boil.

2 Add the flour all at once. Remove from the heat and beat until the mixture leaves the sides of the pan. Allow to cool to room temperature. Stir in the cheese. Beat the eggs then beat in gradually until the mixture is smooth and satiny.

3 Drop teaspoons of batter onto the greased baking sheets. Bake for about 20 minutes or until puffy and golden. Remove from sheets and cool on racks. Cut each puff in half. Scoop out any soft centres. Drain the salmon, discarding any skin and bones and place the salmon in a bowl. Flake with a fork and mix in the mayonnaise and olives. Fill the puffs with the mixture and, if desired, garnish with caviar. Serve immediately.

NOTE: Nutritional figures are for 4–5 puffs and include salt..

NUTRITIONAL INFORMATION	
Kcal	380
Protein	19g
Carbs	12g
Fat	29g
Salt	2.2g
Sodium	880mg

Layered Fish Terrine

[SERVES 4]

450 g/1 lb salmon, skinned and
  boned and cut into long strips
salt and white pepper, to taste
150 ml/5 fl oz medium-bodied dry
  white wine
2 small bunches watercress,
  trimmed
15 g/¹/₂ oz butter

1 shallot, finely chopped
450 g/1 lb firm white fish, such as
  hake, monkfish or cod, skinned,
  boned and cubed
2 egg whites
210 ml/7¹/₂ fl oz double cream,
  chilled

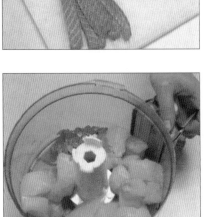

1 Season the salmon lightly and pour over the wine. Cover and chill for 1 hour. Blanch the watercress for 1 minute. Drain, rinse under cold running water, drain again. Dry on kitchen paper; set aside. Heat the butter in a small saucepan. Cook the shallot gently until softened but not browned. Purée with the white fish in a blender.

2 Add the egg whites and season with salt and pepper. Mix for 1 minute, then slowly add the cream. Remove and reserve two thirds of the mixture. Add the watercress to the blender and purée briefly. Chill both mixtures for 30 minutes. Preheat oven to 180C/350F/Gas mk 4. Lightly oil a 25 x 9-cm/10 x 3¹/₂-inch terrine.

3 Spread half the white mixture in the terrine, then half the salmon strips followed by all the green mixture. Cover with remaining salmon strips, then remaining white mixture. Cover with foil, place in a roasting tin and pour in enough boiling water to come halfway up the sides. Bake for 40 minutes, until a skewer inserted in the centre comes out clean. Cool on a wire rack, then refrigerate. Serve cut into slices.

NUTRITIONAL INFORMATION	
Kcal	580
Protein	44g
Carbs	3g
Fat	43g
Salt	0.8g
Sodium	300mg

Gravad Lax

[SERVES 8]

3 tablespoons sea salt
2–3 tablespoons light brown sugar
2 teaspoons crushed black
 peppercorns
6 tablespoons lime juice
1 large bunch of dill, chopped
1.4–1.8 kg/3–4 lb salmon, filleted,
 with skin

DILL AND MUSTARD SAUCE:
3 tablespoons Dijon mustard
2 tablespoons white wine vinegar
1 tablespoon sugar
150 ml/5 fl oz grapeseed oil
2 tablespoons finely chopped
 fresh dill
salt and pepper, to taste

1 In a small bowl, mix together the salt, sugar, peppercorns and lime juice. Spread some dill in a shallow, non-metallic dish and add a quarter of the salt mixture.

2 Lay 1 fillet, skin side down, in the dish. Cover with dill and spoon over half of the remaining salt mixture. Place the other fillet on top, skin-side uppermost. Cover with the dill and pour over the rest of the salt mixture. Cover with greaseproof paper then cling film. Place a 900 g/2 lb weight on top and leave in the bottom of the refrigerator for 3 days, turning occasionally and spooning liquid between the fillets.

3 To make the sauce, mix together the mustard, vinegar and sugar, then gradually whisk in the oil. Add the chopped dill and seasoning. Drain the salmon, pat dry and trim off any hard edges. Slice on the bias into very thin slices, discarding the skin. Serve with the sauce.

NOTE: The salt and sodium values will vary depending on the amount remaining on the fish.

NUTRITIONAL INFORMATION	
Kcal	520
Protein	38g
Carbs	3g
Fat	40g
Salt	1.6g
Sodium	920mg

Tuna Basquaise

[SERVES 6]

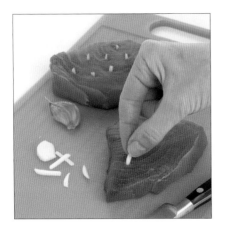

6 slices tuna, about 2½ cm/1 inch
  thick
4 cloves garlic
85 ml/3 fl oz olive oil
1 large onion, finely chopped
1 large red pepper, seeded, cored
  and thinly sliced
1 green pepper, seeded, cored and
  thinly sliced

400 g/14 oz tomatoes, peeled,
  seeded and diced
1 tablespoon sun-dried tomato
  paste
3 sprigs thyme
1 bay leaf
salt and pepper, to taste
salad leaves, for garnish

1 Cut slits in the tuna, then slice 2 cloves of garlic into slivers and insert into the slits. Preheat a griddle pan or grill.

2 Brush the tuna with oil and griddle, or grill, until lightly browned on both sides. Remove tuna from pan or grill and set aside. Heat the remaining oil in a large frying pan, add the onion and peppers and cook over a moderate heat, stirring frequently, for about 10 minutes, until soft. Chop the remaining garlic, add to the pan, cook for 1 minute, then add the tomatoes, tomato paste, thyme and bay leaf. Simmer, uncovered, for 15–20 minutes, stirring occasionally.

3 Add the tuna to the pan, season with salt and pepper, then cover with buttered greaseproof paper and cook gently for 15 minutes. Serve garnished with salad leaves.

NUTRITIONAL INFORMATION	
Kcal	160
Protein	13g
Carbs	6g
Fat	9g
Salt	0.2g
Sodium	60mg

Warm Tuna Niçoise

[SERVES 4]

700 g/1¹/₂ lb small new potatoes
salt and black pepper, to taste
1 tablespoon olive oil, plus extra
    for brushing
450 g/1 lb green beans
4 tuna steaks, about 150 g/5 oz
    each and 1 cm/¹/₂ inch thick
2 tomatoes, quartered
25 g/1 oz Nicoise olives, for garnish

DRESSING:
2 teaspoons wholegrain mustard
1 tablespoon anchovy paste
1 clove garlic, finely chopped
3 tablespoons red wine vinegar
4 tablespoons olive oil
2 teaspoons capers

1 To make the dressing, stir the mustard, anchovy paste, garlic and vinegar together in a bowl, then slowly pour in the oil, whisking constantly. Whisk in the capers; set aside.

2 Boil the potatoes in their skins until tender, drain and then cut into 2-cm/³/₄-inch pieces and place in a bowl. Add the pepper to the dressing and lightly stir 3 tablespoons of the dressing into the potatoes. Heat a large, heavy frying pan, add the olive oil, then the beans. Stir-fry for 5 minutes, until tender but still crisp. Transfer to a bowl and stir in 1 tablespoon dressing. Preheat the grill or griddle pan.

3 Season both sides of the tuna with pepper, brush with oil, then grill or griddle over a moderately high heat for 4 minutes, turning once, until brown outside and slightly rare in the middle. Transfer to a warm serving dish. Add the tomatoes and trickle 1 tablespoon dressing over the top; drizzle the remainder over the tuna. Add the beans and potatoes and scatter the olives over. Serve immediately.

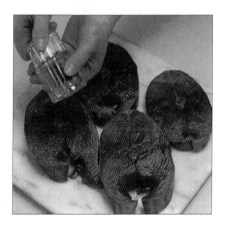

NUTRITIONAL INFORMATION	
Kcal	560
Protein	43g
Carbs	40g
Fat	25g
Salt	1.3g
Sodium	510mg

Tuna with a Ginger Vinaigrette

[SERVES 6]

2¹/2-cm/1-inch piece fresh ginger, peeled and finely chopped
2 large spring onions, white and some green parts, thinly sliced
225 ml/8 fl oz olive oil
juice of 2 limes
2 tablespoons soy sauce
2 tablespoons sesame oil

1 bunch of coriander, finely chopped
black pepper, to taste
6 tuna steaks, about 150–175 g/ 5–6 oz each
leek and red pepper stir-fry with sesame seeds, to serve (optional)
coriander sprigs, for garnish

1 Preheat the grill, if using. To make the vinaigrette, in a small bowl, stir together the ginger, spring onions, olive oil, lime juice and soy sauce, then whisk in the sesame oil. Add the chopped coriander and season with pepper; set aside.

2 Grill or griddle the tuna under a high heat for 3¹/2–4 minutes each side, or a little longer for well done fish. Spoon some of the dressing onto 6 serving plates and add the fish.

3 Serve with a leek and red pepper stir-fry (if liked), garnished with sprigs of coriander. Serve any remaining dressing separately or drizzled over the fish.

NUTRITIONAL INFORMATION	
Kcal	540
Protein	36g
Carbs	1g
Fat	43g
Salt	1.1g
Sodium	450mg

Herrings in Oatmeal

[SERVES 4]

about 1 tablespoon Dijon
  mustard
about 1¹/₂ teaspoons tarragon
  vinegar
85 ml/3 fl oz thick mayonnaise
85 ml/3 fl oz plain yogurt
4 herrings, about 225 g/8 oz
  each, cleaned and heads and
  tails removed
salt and pepper, to taste
1 lemon, halved
115 g/4 oz medium oatmeal
rice and artichoke heart salad,
  to serve
lemon wedges and coriander
  sprigs, for garnish

1 In a small bowl, beat the mustard and vinegar to taste into the mayonnaise and yogurt, then spoon into a small serving bowl and chill lightly. Preheat the grill.

2 Place one fish on a board, cutside down and opened out. Press gently along the backbone with your thumbs. Turn the fish over and carefully lift away the backbone and attached bones. Season with salt and pepper and squeeze the lemon juice over both sides of the fish, then fold in half, skin-side outwards. Repeat with the remaining fish.

3 Coat each fish evenly in oatmeal, pressing it in well but gently. Grill herrings for 3–4 minutes on each side, until brown and crisp and flesh flakes easily. Serve hot with the mustard sauce, accompanied by a rice and artichoke heart salad and garnished with lemon wedges and sprigs of coriander.

NUTRITIONAL INFORMATION	
Kcal	590
Protein	36g
Carbs	23g
Fat	39g
Salt	0.9g
Sodium	350mg

Mackerel with Mustard

[SERVES 4]

2 tablespoons Dijon mustard
4 tablespoons finely chopped
  fresh coriander
2 cloves garlic, finely crushed
2–3 teaspoons lemon juice
salt and pepper, to taste
4 mackerel, about 300 g/10 oz
  each
rolled oats
tomato and lamb's lettuce salad,
  to serve
lemon wedges and coriander
  sprigs, for garnish

1 Preheat the grill. In a bowl, mix together the mustard, coriander, garlic and lemon juice and season with salt and pepper.

2 Using the point of a sharp knife, cut 3 slashes on each side of the mackerel. Spoon the mustard mixture into the slashes and sprinkle with a few rolled oats. Wrap each fish in a large piece of foil and fold the edges of the foil together to seal tightly.

3 Place the foil packages under a hot grill for 5 minutes. Open the foil, turn the fish and reseal the packages. Cook for a further 2–3 minutes. Open the foil, place the fish directly under the grill and cook for a further 2–3 minutes, until cooked. Serve with a tomato and lamb's lettuce salad, garnished with lemon wedges.

NUTRITIONAL INFORMATION	
Kcal	530
Protein	41g
Carbs	16g
Fat	34g
Salt	0.7g
Sodium	270mg

Mackerel with Yogurt

[SERVES 4]

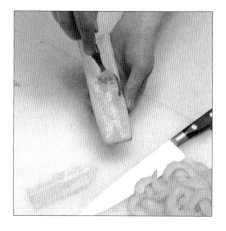

1/2 cucumber, peeled
salt and pepper, to taste
175 ml/6 fl oz plain thick yogurt,
  preferably Greek style
1 1/4 tablespoons chopped fresh
  mint
1 clove garlic, finely crushed
1/2 teaspoon harissa or pinch of
  chilli powder

2 teaspoons ground cumin
2 tablespoons light olive oil
squeeze of lemon juice
4 mackerel, cleaned
chicory, bean and red onion salad,
  to serve

1 Halve the cucumber lengthways and scoop out the seeds. Thinly slice the flesh and spread in a colander. Sprinkle with salt and leave to drain for 30 minutes. Rinse the cucumber, dry with kitchen paper, then mix with the yogurt and mint. Cover and chill for 2 hours.

2 Place the garlic in a mortar, or small bowl, then pound in the harissa or chilli powder, cumin and oil, using a pestle or the end of a rolling pin. Add the lemon juice and season with salt and pepper.

3 With the point of a sharp knife, cut slashes in each side of the fish. Spread the spice mixture over the fish, cover and leave for 15–30 minutes. Preheat the grill and cook the fish for 7–8 minutes on each side. Serve with the cucumber mixture, accompanied by a chicory, bean and red onion salad.

NUTRITIONAL INFORMATION	
Kcal	530
Protein	41g
Carbs	4g
Fat	40g
Salt	0.8g
Sodium	300mg

Sardines in Coriander Sauce

[SERVES 4]

4 tablespoons olive oil
grated rind of 1¹/₂ limes
1¹/₂ tablespoons lime juice
³/₄ teaspoon finely crushed,
  toasted coriander seeds
3 tablespoons chopped fresh
  coriander
salt and pepper, to taste
1 kg/2 lb sardines (at least 12)
lamb's lettuce, for garnish
lime wedges, to serve

1 Thoroughly whisk together the oil, lime rind and juice, coriander seeds, chopped coriander and salt and pepper.

2 Place the sardines in a shallow, non-metallic dish. Pour the coriander mixture over, cover and leave to marinate for 1 hour, turning the sardines over once.

3 Preheat the grill. Remove the sardines from the marinade and grill for 4–5 minutes on each side, basting with the coriander mixture. Serve the sardines garnished with lamb's lettuce and accompanied by lime wedges.

NUTRITIONAL INFORMATION	
Kcal	380
Protein	21g
Carbs	Trace
Fat	33g
Salt	0.3g
Sodium	120mg

Stuffed Sardines

[SERVES 4]

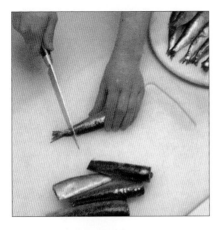

12 sardines, cleaned
1 tablespoon each chopped fresh
   parsley, chives, dill, basil and 2
   small sage leaves, chopped
1 clove garlic
25 g/1 oz pine nuts, lightly
   toasted
pinch of crushed, dried chillies

2 tablespoons light virgin olive oil
salt and pepper, to taste
1/2 lemon
2 1/2 tablespoons fresh
   breadcrumbs
grilled baby vegetables and lemon
   wedges, to serve

1 Preheat oven to 220C/425F/Gas mk 7. Oil a wide, shallow baking dish. Cut the heads and tails from the sardines. Slit along the underside of the bodies to open them out. Discard the intestines, wash the cavities and then pat dry with kitchen paper.

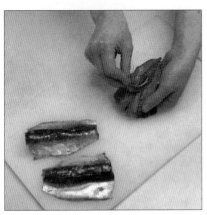

2 Lay 1 fish, skin side uppermost, on a work surface then, using your thumbs, press gently along the centre of the back to dislodge the backbone. Turn the fish over and gently pull away the backbone. Repeat with the remaining sardines.

3 Finely chop the herbs, garlic and nuts, then mix with the crushed chillies, 1 tablespoon oil and salt and pepper. Lay 6 sardines, skin side down, in a single layer in the dish. Squeeze over some lemon juice, then spread some of the herb mixture on each fish. Cover with the remaining sardines, skin side up. Sprinkle with breadcrumbs, then drizzle the remaining oil over the top. Bake for about 10 minutes, until golden. Serve hot or at room temperature with baby vegetables and lemon wedges.

NUTRITIONAL INFORMATION	
Kcal	410
Protein	23g
Carbs	4g
Fat	34g
Salt	0.3g
Sodium	120mg

MIXED CATCH

Anchovy Beignets

[MAKES 12–15]

55 g/2 oz butter
125 ml/4 fl oz water
55 g/2 oz plain flour
4 canned anchovy fillets,
   drained and mashed
2 eggs
25 g/1oz slivered almonds
vegetable oil, for deep-frying

1 Cut the butter into cubes and put into a saucepan with the water. Heat until the butter melts, then bring to the boil.

2 Add the flour all at once and stir for about 1 minute, until the paste leaves the side of the saucepan. Cool. Transfer to a bowl. Beat in the anchovy fillets and eggs, add a little at a time, until the mixture is glossy. Stir in the slivered almonds.

3 Heat the oil in a medium saucepan. When hot drop a few teaspoonfuls of the anchovy mixture into the oil. Cook a few at a time for about 5 minutes, until golden. Remove with a slotted spoon and drain on absorbent kitchen paper. Repeat until all the batter is used. Serve hot.

NUTRITIONAL INFORMATION	
Kcal	120
Protein	1g
Carbs	4g
Fat	11g
Salt	0.3g
Sodium	100mg

Spicy Fish Balls

[MAKES 24]

450 g/1 lb white fish fillets
1 teaspoon grated fresh ginger
1¹/₂ teaspoons curry powder
1 teaspoon salt
4 spring onions, finely chopped
3 eggs
125g/4 oz dry bread crumbs
3 tablespoons sesame seeds
vegetable oil, for frying
lemon slices and plain yogurt, to
  serve

1   Poach fish fillets in water until cooked. Allow fish to cool. Flake the fish, removing any skin and bones.

2   Put the fish into a bowl with the ginger, curry powder, salt and spring onions. Beat 1 of the eggs and add to the fish. Mix well with a fork and form the mixture into 24 small balls.

3   Mix the breadcrumbs with the sesame seeds. Beat the remaining eggs in a shallow dish. Roll the fish balls in the eggs, then in the breadcrumbs. Pour oil to 1-cm/¹/₂-inch depth in a heavy-based frying pan. Heat oil and fry the fishballs until golden. Drain on kitchen paper. Serve warm with lemon slices and, if liked, yogurt for dipping.

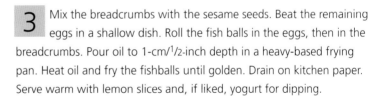

NUTRITIONAL INFORMATION	
Kcal	90
Protein	6g
Carbs	4g
Fat	5g
Salt	0.4g
Sodium	150g

Sushi with Shrimp

[MAKES 24]

450 g/1 lb short-grain rice
600 ml/20 fl oz water
2 tablespoons mirin (sweet sake)
4 tablespoons rice vinegar
2 tablespoons sugar
2 teaspoons salt

24 cooked Mediterranean (king)
  prawns
2 teaspoons wasabi powder
nori (dried laver seaweed), if
  desired

1   Wash the rice several times in cold water and allow to drain well
    for 30 minutes. Put into a saucepan with the cold water. Bring to
the boil, cover and steam over very low heat for 15 minutes. Heat mirin,
vinegar, sugar and salt until boiling. Cool.

2   Remove rice from the heat and leave for 10 minutes. Turn rice
    into a large shallow dish and pour the vinegar dressing over. Mix
gently but thoroughly until the rice reaches room temperature.

3   Shape the sushi into neat ovals and place on a serving platter.
    Peel the prawns, removing heads and leaving on the tails. Split
down the underside - not all the way through - and flatten out. Mix the
powder with a few drops of water. Dab a little on the rice ovals and top
each with a prawn. Wrap a strip of seaweed around each sushi, if
desired.

NOTE: Wasabi is a very hot horseradish powder available from Asian
food stores.

NUTRITIONAL INFORMATION	
Kcal	90
Protein	4g
Carbs	18g
Fat	Trace
Salt	0.4g
Sodium	160mg

John Dory with Orange

[SERVES 4]

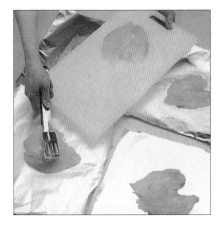

4 John Dory fillets, about
165 g/5¹/₂ oz each
4 sprigs mint
4 tablespoons dry white vermouth
finely grated rind and juice of 1
orange
1–2 tablespoons virgin olive oil
salt and pepper, to taste
orange slices, for garnish

1 Preheat oven to 180C/350F/Gas mk 4. Cut 4 pieces of foil, each large enough to enclose 1 piece of fish. Oil the top side of each piece then place a fish fillet in the centre of each piece.

2 Pinch out the centre of each mint sprig and reserve for garnish. Finely chop the remaining mint. In a small bowl, mix the chopped mint with the vermouth, orange rind and juice, olive oil and salt and pepper.

3 Fold up the sides of the foil parcels, spoon one quarter of the orange mixture over each fish, then seal the edges of the foil tightly. Place the foil parcels on a baking tray and bake for 12–15 minutes. Serve garnished with orange slices and the reserved mint.

NUTRITIONAL INFORMATION	
Kcal	200
Protein	29g
Carbs	3g
Fat	6g
Salt	0.3g
Sodium	130mg

Fish & Watercress Sauce

[SERVES 4]

4 John Dory, brill or porgy fillets,
   about 175 g/6 oz each, skinned
mixed salad, to serve

SAUCE:
25 g/1 oz unsalted butter
leaves and fine stems of 1 large
   bunch watercress
150 ml/5 fl oz mayonnaise
about 1 tablespoon lemon juice
salt and pepper, to taste

1 Bring the base of a steamer filled with water to the boil. Lay the fish fillets in a steaming basket, cover, place over the steamer base and steam for about 5 minutes.

2 Meanwhile, make the sauce. In a medium saucepan, heat the butter, add the watercress and sauté for 2–3 minutes.

3 Transfer the watercress and butter to a blender, add the mayonnaise and mix briefly. With the motor running, slowly trickle in 1 tablespoon lemon juice. Season with salt and pepper and add extra lemon juice if necessary. Season the fish and serve with a mixed salad, accompanied by the watercress sauce.

NUTRITIONAL INFORMATION	
Kcal	450
Protein	30g
Carbs	Trace
Fat	36g
Salt	0.6g
Sodium	230g

155

Bream Duglere

[SERVES 4]

4 bream fillets, about 175 g/6 oz
  each
salt and pepper, to taste
250 ml/9 fl oz fish stock
6 tablespoons medium-bodied dry
  white wine
150 ml/5 fl oz double cream
1 large sun-ripened beefsteak
  tomato, peeled, seeded and cut
  into 1-cm/½-inch strips
basil or parsley sprigs, for garnish

1 Season the fish, then place in a single layer in a well buttered frying pan. Add the stock and wine and bring just to the boil. Reduce the heat, cover and poach the fish for 4–6 minutes.

2 Using a fish slice, transfer the fish to a warm plate, cover and keep warm. Boil the cooking liquid rapidly until reduced to a quarter. Stir the cream into the pan and simmer for 2–3 minutes.

3 Add the tomato strips and heat gently for 1 minute. Season the sauce, then pour over the fish. Serve garnished with basil or parsley sprigs.

NUTRITIONAL INFORMATION	
Kcal	310
Protein	31g
Carbs	2g
Fat	19g
Salt	0.4g
Sodium	150mg

Baked Bream with Fennel

[SERVES 4–6]

2 fennel bulbs, thinly sliced
1 red onion, thinly sliced
3 cloves garlic, sliced
1 lemon, peeled and thinly sliced
3 small sprigs rosemary, plus extra
  for garnish
2 sea bream, about 575 g/1¼ lb
  each, cleaned and scaled
1 tablespoon fennel seeds,
  cracked
salt and pepper, to taste
5 tablespoons olive oil

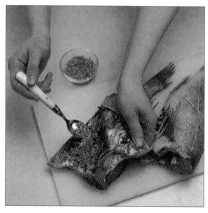

1 Preheat oven to 180C/350F/Gas mk 4. Spread the sliced fennel, onion, garlic, lemon and rosemary in a baking dish large enough to hold the fish. Cook in the oven for about 8 minutes.

2 Meanwhile, with the point of a sharp knife, cut slashes in each side of the fish and put half the fennel seeds inside each fish.

3 Place the fish on the vegetables in the baking dish. Season with salt and pepper and pour the oil over them. Bake for 20–25 minutes, turning halfway through, until the vegetables and fish are tender. Serve garnished with rosemary sprigs.

NUTRITIONAL INFORMATION	
Kcal	290
Protein	28g
Carbs	5g
Fat	18g
Salt	0.3g
Sodium	130mg

Bream with Lemon & Herbs

[SERVES 4]

2 tablespoons chopped fresh
  mixed herbs, such as thyme,
  rosemary, marjoram, fennel and
  basil
1/2 clove garlic, chopped
juice of 1/2 lemon
salt and pepper, to taste
3 tablespoons extra virgin olive oil
4 bream fillets, about 250 g/9 oz
  each
finely grated lemon rind and slices
  and parsley sprigs, for garnish

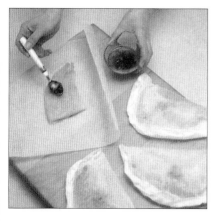

1 Preheat oven to 200C/400F/Gas mk 6. Briefly chop together the herbs and garlic. Place in a bowl, stir in the lemon juice, season with salt and pepper, then gradually beat in the oil using a fork so that the mixture thickens; set aside.

2 Cut 4 pieces of greaseproof paper, each large enough to enclose a fish fillet. Place 1 fillet on each piece of paper and spoon over the herb mixture. Fold the paper loosely over the fish and tightly seal the edges.

3 Place the parcels on a baking tray and cook for about 15 minutes. Serve the fish in the paper parcels, garnished with lemon rind and slices and parsley sprigs.

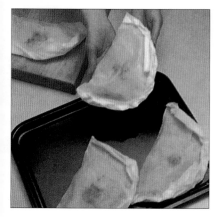

NUTRITIONAL INFORMATION	
Kcal	280
Protein	44g
Carbs	0g
Fat	12g
Salt	0.5g
Sodium	190mg

Chinese Style Bream

[SERVES 2]

4 tablespoons soy sauce
1 carrot, cut into fine strips
3 spring onions, cut into fine strips
2¹/₂-cm/1-inch piece fresh ginger,
   peeled and finely shredded
575 g/1¹/₄ lb bream fillets
2 tablespoons sesame oil
2 tablespoons groundnut oil
1 fresh red chilli, cut into rings,
   seeded
1 clove garlic, shredded
chopped fresh chives, for garnish

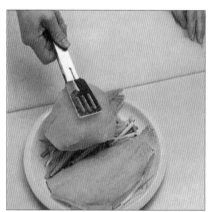

1 Put a little of the soy sauce on a large serving plate. Mix together the carrot, spring onions and ginger and use half of the mixture to make a bed on a plate for the fish.

2 Place the fish on top of the vegetables. Scatter over the remaining vegetables, then trickle over the remaining soy sauce. Place the plate in a steaming basket. Fill the bottom of the steamer with water and bring to the boil. Put the basket on the steamer and cook for 10–14 minutes.

3 Meanwhile, in a small saucepan, very gently heat the sesame and groundnut oils. Add the chilli and garlic and cook for 5–7 minutes. Remove the plate from the steaming basket, baste the fish with the cooking juices, then pour over the hot oil, garlic and chilli. Garnish with chopped chives.

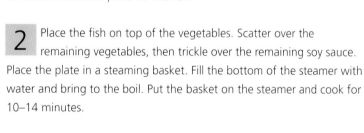

NUTRITIONAL INFORMATION	
Kcal	490
Protein	52g
Carbs	6g
Fat	28g
Salt	5.1g
Sodium	2000mg

Fish Plaki

[SERVES 4]

about 1.2 kg/1³/4 lb fish, such as
  bream, bass, grey mullet, red
  snapper or pompano, scaled
juice of ¹/2 lemon
2 tablespoons olive oil
1 onion, chopped
1 carrot, finely chopped
1 stick celery, chopped
2 cloves garlic, chopped
1 teaspoon coriander seeds,
  crushed

450 g/1 lb tomatoes, peeled,
  seeded and chopped
3 halves sun-dried tomato, finely
  chopped
85 ml/3 fl oz dry white wine
leaves from 1 bunch of parsley,
  finely chopped
salt and pepper, to taste
parsley sprigs, for garnish

1 Preheat oven to 190C/375F/Gas mk 5. Place the fish in a baking dish and squeeze over the lemon juice. Heat the oil in a saucepan, add the onion, carrot and celery and cook, stirring occasionally, until the onion has softened but not coloured.

2 Stir in the garlic and cook for about 3 minutes. Add the coriander seeds, tomatoes, sun-dried tomatoes, wine and parsley, stir, then season with salt and pepper and simmer for a few minutes, until well blended.

3 Using a fish slice, lift the fish and pour about a quarter of the tomato mixture underneath. Lay the fish down again and pour over the remaining tomato mixture. Cover and bake in the oven for about 40 minutes. Serve garnished with parsley sprigs.

NUTRITIONAL INFORMATION	
Kcal	400
Protein	67
Carbs	9g
Fat	10g
Salt	0.8g
Sodium	320mg

Skate with Anchovy Sauce

[SERVES 4]

4 small skate wings
1 tablespoon olive oil
15 g/¹/₂ oz unsalted butter
salt and pepper, to taste
sugar snap peas and new
   potatoes, to serve
basil sprigs, for garnish

SAUCE:
1 large clove garlic
6 anchovy fillets, chopped

2¹/₂ tablespoons capers
2¹/₂ teaspoons wholegrain
   mustard
1¹/₂ tablespoons chopped fresh
   basil
3 tablespoons chopped fresh
   parsley
6 teaspoons lime juice
3 tablespoons virgin olive oil
black pepper, to taste

1 To make the sauce, crush the garlic with the anchovies in a small bowl. Mix in the capers, mustard, basil, parsley and lime juice, then gradually whisk in the oil. Season with pepper and set aside.

2 Season the skate wings. In a large non-stick frying pan, heat the oil and butter. Add 2 skate wings and fry for about 4 minutes on each side, until lightly browned.

3 Transfer the fish to kitchen paper and fry the remaining skate in the same way. Return the fish to the pan, pour in the sauce and heat briefly until warmed through. Serve with sugar snap peas and new potatoes, garnished with sprigs of basil.

NUTRITIONAL INFORMATION	
Kcal	280
Protein	28g
Carbs	1g
Fat	19g
Salt	1.2g
Sodium	470mg

Stir-Fried Squid

[SERVES 4]

1 kg/2 lb 4 oz small squid
1¹/₂ tablespoons groundnut oil
2 cloves garlic, slivered
1-cm/¹/₂-inch piece ginger, peeled and finely chopped
2 plump stalks lemon grass, finely crushed and chopped

4 spring onions, white and some green parts, sliced
1 tablespoon rice wine or medium dry sherry
1 tablespoon chopped fresh parsley and basil
lemon wedges, for garnish

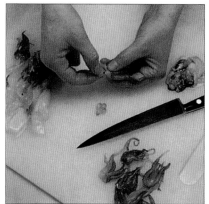

1 Hold the head of each squid in turn, just below the eyes, and gently pull from the body pouch; the soft innards including the ink sac will come with it. Discard the innards.

2 Pull back the rim of the body pouch to locate the fine quill-shaped pen. Carefully pull out and discard. Cut the head from the tentacles just below the eyes and discard the head. Cut out the small round of cartilage at the base of the tentacles and chop the rest. Squeeze the beak-like mouth in the centre of the tentacles to remove. Slip your fingers under the skin of the body pouch, peel off then cut the edible fins from the body. Rinse the squid under cold water, dry and thinly slice.

3 In a preheated wok or large frying pan, heat the oil. Add the garlic, ginger and lemon grass and cook gently for 1 minute. Increase the heat, add the squid and stir fry for 1 minute. Lower the heat, add the spring onions and cook for a further minute. Add the wine, heat briefly, then sprinkle with chopped parsley and basil. To serve, garnish with lemon wedges.

NUTRITIONAL INFORMATION	
Kcal	240
Protein	39g
Carbs	2g
Fat	7g
Salt	1.1g
Sodium	440mg

Stuffed Squid

[SERVES 4]

about 12 small squid
4 tablespoons olive oil
1 small onion, finely chopped
2 cloves garlic, chopped
4 spring onions, chopped
4 anchovy fillets, chopped
6 tomatoes, peeled, seeded and
  chopped

2 tablespoons chopped mixed
  herbs
2 tablespoons fresh breadcrumbs
2 egg yolks
salt and pepper
1 lemon, halved
lemon and cucumber slices and
  chervil sprigs, for garnish

1 Prepare squid as for Stir-Fried Squid (page 169) but do not slice the bodies.

2 In a frying pan, heat 1 tablespoon oil, add the onion, garlic, spring onions and squid tentacles and cook until the onions are tender. Stir in the anchovies, tomatoes, herbs and breadcrumbs and cook, stirring, for 1 minute, then remove from the heat and stir in the egg yolks. Season with plenty of pepper.

3 Preheat oven to 180C/350F/Gas mk 4. Oil a shallow baking dish. Divide the herb mixture between the squid bodies, taking care not to overfill them. Close the opening with wooden cocktail sticks. Place the squid in a single layer in the prepared baking dish, squeeze the lemon juice over them, sprinkle with the remaining oil and season. Bake in the oven for about 20 minutes, until tender, basting with cooking juices occasionally. Serve garnished with lemon and cucumber slices and chervil sprigs.

NUTRITIONAL INFORMATION	
Kcal	400
Protein	43g
Carbs	11g
Fat	19g
Salt	1.7g
Sodium	680mg

Turkish Swordfish Kebabs

[SERVES 4]

575 g/1¹/₄ lb swordfish or
   monkfish
pasta, to serve
lime wedges and parsley sprigs,
   for garnish

MARINADE:
4 tablespoons lemon juice
4 tablespoons olive oil
1 shallot, finely chopped
3 fresh bay leaves, torn

1¹/₂ teaspoons paprika
salt and pepper, to taste

LEMON SAUCE:
3 tablespoons olive oil
3 tablespoons lemon juice
3 tablespoons chopped fresh
   parsley

1 Cut the swordfish or monkfish into 2¹/₂ x 4-cm/1 x 1¹/₂-inch cubes. To prepare marinade, mix the ingredients together in a small bowl; set aside. Lay the fish in a single layer in a wide, shallow, non-metallic dish.

2 Pour over the marinade and turn the fish so it is evenly coated. Cover and leave to marinate in the refridgerator for 4–5 hours, turning occasionally.

3 Meanwhile, mix together the sauce ingredients and season with salt and pepper; set aside. Preheat a grill or barbecue. Oil the grill rack. Remove the fish from the marinade and thread onto 4 skewers. Grill or barbecue the kebabs for 4–5 minutes on each side, basting frequently. Serve with the sauce on a bed of pasta, garnished with lime wedges and sprigs of parsley.

NUTRITIONAL INFORMATION	
Kcal	220
Protein	24g
Carbs	Trace
Fat	14g
Salt	0.4g
Sodium	170mg

Swordfish with Tomatoes

[SERVES 4]

3 tablespoons olive oil
4 swordfish steaks
1 small onion, finely chopped
2 cloves garlic, crushed
575 g/1¼ lb tomatoes, skinned,
  seeded and chopped
2 halves sun-dried tomatoes,
  finely chopped
2 tablespoons chopped fresh
  parsley

1 bay leaf, torn
black pepper, to taste
8 oil-cured black olives, halved
  and stoned
rice, to serve
1 tablespoon chopped fresh
  parsley
courgette batons, to serve
basil sprigs, for garnish

1 To prepare the fish, heat half the oil in a frying pan (or preheat a griddle pan and brush the fish with oil). Add the fish to the pan and cook quickly to brown on both sides. Transfer to a plate.

2 Heat the remaining oil in the frying pan, add the onion and garlic and cook until softened but not coloured. Add in the chopped tomatoes, sun-dried tomatoes, chopped parsley and bay leaf, stir for about 1 minute, then boil until thickened.

3 Season the tomato mixture with pepper, add the fish and baste with the sauce. Cook gently, turning the fish once, for 10–15 minutes, until the fish is cooked through. Just before the end of the cooking time, scatter the olives over the top. Prepare the rice as directed on the packet and then mix in the chopped fresh parsley. Serve the fish with the rice and courgette batons, garnished with sprigs of basil.

NUTRITIONAL INFORMATION	
Kcal	240
Protein	27g
Carbs	8g
Fat	12g
Salt	0.9g
Sodium	340mg

Escabeche

[SERVES 6–8 AS A FIRST COURSE]

6–8 red snapper, red sea bream or
  catfish fillets, cleaned and scaled
3 tablespoons seasoned flour
3 tablespoons olive oil
2–3 tablespoons chopped fresh
  coriander

MARINADE:
large pinch of saffron threads,
  toasted
2 tablespoons olive oil

2 red onions, thinly sliced
2 red peppers, seeded and sliced
1/2 teaspoon dried chilli flakes
1 1/2 teaspoons cumin seeds, lightly
  crushed
finely grated rind and juice of 1
  orange
2–3 tablespoons rice vinegar
pinch of caster sugar
salt and pepper, to taste

1 To make the marinade, crush the saffron threads, then soak in warm water for 10 minutes. In a frying pan, heat the oil and gently cook onions for 2 minutes.

2 Add the peppers, chilli flakes and cumin and fry until the vegetables are soft. Stir in the saffron and liquid, orange rind and juice, vinegar, sugar and salt and pepper. Bubble for a few minutes, then leave to cool.

3 Toss the fish in flour. In a frying pan, heat the oil, add the fish and fry for 2–3 minutes on each side, until just cooked and browned. Place in a single layer in a shallow, non-metallic dish and pour over the marinade. Cover and chill for 4–12 hours. Return to room temperature 15 minutes before serving and stir in the coriander.

NOTE: Garnish with orange slices and sprigs of coriander, if desired.

NUTRITIONAL INFORMATION	
Kcal	200
Protein	22g
Carbs	6g
Fat	10g
Salt	0.2g
Sodium	90mg

Cajun-Style Red Snapper

[SERVES 2]

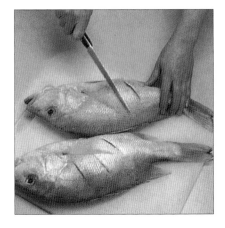

2 red snapper, about 575–700 g/
  1 1/4–1 1/2 lb each
25 g/1 oz unsalted butter
2 tablespoons olive oil
lemon and lime slices to serve
  (optional)
green salad, to serve (optional)

SPICE MIX:
1 plump clove garlic
1/2 onion
1 teaspoon salt
1 teaspoon paprika
1/2 teaspoon cayenne pepper
1/2 teaspoon ground cumin
1/2 teaspoon mustard powder
1 teaspoon each dried thyme and
  dried oregano
1/2 teaspoon pepper

1 With the point of a sharp knife, cut 3 slashes on each side of both fish.

2 To make the spice mix, crush together the garlic and onion with salt in a pestle and mortar or in a bowl using the end of a rolling pin. Stir in the remaining spice mix ingredients. Spread some of the spice mix over each fish, making sure it goes into the slashes. Lay the fish in a shallow dish, cover and leave in a cool place for 1 hour.

3 In a large frying pan, heat the butter and oil until sizzling. Add the fish and fry for about 4 minutes on each side, until the fish is cooked and the spice coating has blackened. Serve with lemon and lime slices and a green salad, if liked.

NUTRITIONAL INFORMATION	
Kcal	340
Protein	52g
Carbs	0g
Fat	15g
Salt	3.0g
Sodium	1200mg

Red Snapper with Mushrooms

[SERVES 4]

175 g/6 oz mushrooms
4 spring onions
2 (700-g/1¹/₂-lb) red snapper or 1
1 (1¹/₂-kg/3-lb) grouper, cleaned
   and scaled but with head and
   tail left on
2¹/₂ tablespoons chopped fresh
   coriander
1 tablespoon olive oil

1 tablespoon melted butter
2 tablespoons lemon juice
300 ml/10 fl oz medium-bodied
   dry white wine
150 ml/5 fl oz freshly squeezed
   tangerine juice
salt and pepper, to taste
tangerine wedges, for garnish

1 Preheat oven to 200C/400F/Gas mk 6. Butter a baking dish just large enough to hold the fish. Slice the mushrooms and finely chop the spring onions (green and white parts).

2 Scatter the mushrooms and spring onions in the bottom of the dish, place the fish on top and then sprinkle over the chopped coriander. Mix together the oil, butter, lemon juice, wine and tangerine juice and season with salt and pepper. Pour the mixture over the fish.

3 Bake for 20–30 minutes, until the flesh flakes when tested. If cooking juices are too thin, transfer the fish and vegetables to a warm serving plate and keep warm. Pour the juices into a pan and boil to concentrate slightly, then pour them over the fish. Serve garnished with tangerine wedges.

NUTRITIONAL INFORMATION	
Kcal	210
Protein	32g
Carbs	4g
Fat	5g
Salt	0.4g
Sodium	140mg

Swordfish with Courgette Sauce

[SERVES 4]

3¹/₂ tablespoons olive oil
1 clove garlic, finely chopped
300 g/10 oz courgettes, diced
2 tablespoons fish stock or dry
  white wine
2 swordfish steaks, halved, or 4
  mahi mahi fillets
10 basil leaves

1 large tomato, peeled, seeded
  and chopped
rice, to serve
1 tablespoon chopped fresh
  parsley
salt and pepper, to taste
basil sprigs, for garnish

1 In a frying pan, heat the oil, add the garlic and cook gently until golden. Add the courgettes and the stock or wine.

2 Place the fish on the courgettes and place the basil leaves and tomato on top of the fish. Cover the pan tightly and cook gently for 10 minutes. Meanwhile, prepare the rice as directed on the packet and then mix in the chopped fresh parsley; set aside. Transfer the fish, with the tomato, to warm plates. Season with salt and pepper, cover and keep warm.

3 If necessary, continue to cook the courgettes until tender. Transfer to a blender or food processor and blend with the basil and garlic. With the motor running, slowly pour in 1–2 tablespoons oil and sufficient cooking water to make a soft purée. Season and then divide the courgette purée between the fish. Serve with rice, garnished with sprigs of basil.

NUTRITIONAL INFORMATION	
Kcal	170
Protein	14g
Carbs	1g
Fat	12g
Salt	0.2g
Sodium	90mg

SEAFOOD
DISHES

Artichokes with Caviar

[MAKES 6]

1 (400-g/14-oz) tin artichoke
   bottoms
3–6 slices white bread
2 tablespoons vegetable oil
2 tablespoons thick sour cream
1 tablespoon aioli or homemade
   mayonnaise
juice of $\frac{1}{2}$ lemon
1 tablespoon snipped fresh
   chives
6 teaspoons black or red caviar
dill sprigs, for garnish

1 Drain the artichoke bottoms, discarding the liquid in the tin.

2 Cut out 6 rounds of bread using a biscuit cutter. Heat the oil in a shallow pan. When hot, fry the bread rounds until golden on both sides. Drain on absorbent kitchen paper. Combine the sour cream and aioli, adding a few drops of lemon juice to taste, then stir in the snipped chives.

3 To serve, place the artichoke bottoms on the bread rounds, top with a spoonful of the sour cream mixture and the caviar, and garnish with dill.

NOTE: The bread can be prepared 24 hours in advance and stored in an airtight container and the cream can be mixed and chilled ready to assemble at the last moment.

NUTRITIONAL INFORMATION	
Kcal	150
Protein	3g
Carbs	14g
Fat	8g
Salt	0.5g
Sodium	200mg

Caviar Croutons

[MAKES 20]

10 slices white bread
2 tablespoons vegetable oil
25 g/1 oz butter
1–2 teaspoons bottled hot
  horseradish
125 ml/4 fl oz thick sour cream
3 tablespoons red salmon roe
fresh parsley sprigs, for garnish
  (optional)

1 To make the croutons, cut shapes out of sliced bread. Use shaped cutters for hearts and cut diamonds with a knife. Trimmings can be used for making breadcrumbs.

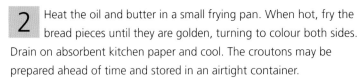

2 Heat the oil and butter in a small frying pan. When hot, fry the bread pieces until they are golden, turning to colour both sides. Drain on absorbent kitchen paper and cool. The croutons may be prepared ahead of time and stored in an airtight container.

3 Stir the horseradish into the sour cream, adding more to taste if preferred. Just before serving, spoon the sour cream onto the croutons and top with the salmon roe. Garnish with parsley sprigs, if desired.

NUTRITIONAL INFORMATION	
Kcal	80
Protein	2g
Carbs	9g
Fat	4g
Salt	0.3g
Sodium	110mg

Caviar Moulds

[MAKES 4 SMALL MOULDS OR 1 LARGE MOULD]

250 g/9 oz black caviar
2 teaspoons gelatine
125 ml/4 fl oz boiling water
300 ml/10 fl oz carton thick sour
  cream
3 spring onions, finely chopped
hard-boiled eggs and fresh
  herbs (optional), for garnish
melba toast, to serve (optional)

1 Put the caviar in a bowl. Dissolve the gelatine in the boiling water. Allow to cool but not set. Stir into the caviar.

2 Divide the caviar mixture between four small moulds or pour into one large mould. Chill until set. Meanwhile, combine the sour cream with the spring onions. Cover and chill until needed.

3 Unmould the caviar mousse by dipping the moulds into hot water and turning upside down on to a serving platter. Garnish with cut-out shapes of hardboiled egg whites, sieved yolks, and sprigs of fresh herbs. Serve with the sour cream sauce and melba toast, if liked.

NOTE: For the best results do not make the caviar mousse more than 24 hours before serving. The figures given below are for 1 of 4 small moulds, without egg garnish.

NUTRITIONAL INFORMATION	
Kcal	220
Protein	10g
Carbs	3g
Fat	13g
Salt	0.3g
Sodium	110g

Celery with Shrimp

[MAKES ABOUT 18]

300 ml/10 fl oz thick sour cream
1 tablespoon drained capers
1 tablespoon snipped fresh chives
2 tablespoons mild French
mustard
450 g /lb medium cooked prawns
3 or 4 sticks celery

1 Drain any liquid from the sour cream. If the cream is thin, whisk until it thickens. Chop the capers and add to the cream with the chives and mustard. Mix well. Chill.

2 Peel and de-vein the prawns. If large, cut each into 2 or 3 pieces.

3 Trim the celery and cut into 5-cm/2-in lengths. Trim the rib off each length of celery so it will sit flat. Make sure the celery is well chilled and crisp. Spoon the sour cream mixture into each celery length and top with the prawns. Serve immediately.

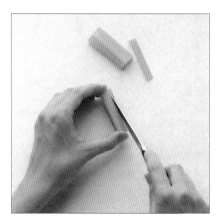

NUTRITIONAL INFORMATION	
Kcal	70
Protein	7g
Carbs	1g
Fat	4g
Salt	1.2g
Sodium	460mg

Cantonese Prawns

[SERVES 4–6]

1 orange
2 tablespoons soy sauce
2 tablespoons clear honey
2 tablespoons dry sherry
2 tablespoons white wine
  vinegar
1 teaspoon five spice powder
700 g/1½ lb raw king prawns,
  peeled and deveined
spring onion slices, for garnish

1 With a vegetable peeler or small sharp knife, remove 6 strips of zest from the orange, taking care not to include any white pith.

2 Cut the strips into fine shreds, add to a small saucepan of boiling water and blanch for 2 minutes. Drain, then put into an empty pan with the soy sauce, honey, sherry, vinegar and five spice powder. Squeeze the juice from the orange and add to the pan. Simmer for 3–4 minutes, then allow to cool.

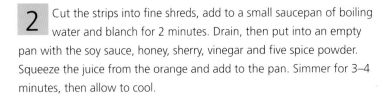

3 Place the prawns in a shallow dish, pour over the orange and soy mixture, cover and leave to stand for 1 hour. In a frying pan, stir-fry the prawns in the sauce for 2–4 minutes, until pink and fully cooked. Serve garnished with spring onion slices.

NUTRITIONAL INFORMATION	
Kcal	200
Protein	31g
Carbs	10g
Fat	2g
Salt	2.0g
Sodium	770mg

VARIATION: Use pomfret or pompano instead of prawns.

Grilled Prawns in Ginger Wine

[MAKES 8]

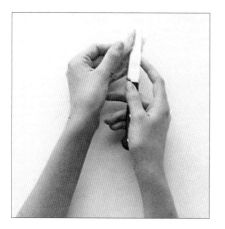

8 raw king prawns, peeled
1 teaspoon olive or vegetable oil
2 tablespoons soy sauce
2 tablespoons ginger wine or
  dry sherry
squeeze of lemon juice
lemon slices, to serve

1 Remove the heads from the prawns. Cut each prawn along the back, taking care not to cut all the way through. Remove the vein.

2 Open the prawns out flat and push a skewer through to hold each prawn open. Mix the oil, soy sauce, ginger wine and lemon juice together in a small bowl.

3 Brush the prawns with the soy sauce mixture. Grill on a barbecue or under a hot grill, basting constantly with the soy mixture until the prawns are cooked and well glazed. Alternatively, fry the prawns in an oiled frying pan, brushing with the soy mixture. Serve whole or cut into pieces with lemon slices.

NUTRITIONAL INFORMATION	
Kcal	30
Protein	4g
Carbs	Trace
Fat	1g
Salt	0.8g
Sodium	300mg

Shrimp Vol-au-Vents

[MAKES 36]

25 g/1 oz butter
2 tablespoons plain flour
315 ml/11 fl oz milk
55 g/2 oz peeled prawns, chopped
squeeze of lemon juice
2 teaspoons snipped fresh chives
pinch of cayenne pepper
1 teaspoon paprika
salt, to taste
36 cocktail vol-au-vent (oyster)
  cases

1 Melt the butter in a saucepan, add the flour and stir well over a low heat for 2 minutes. Remove from heat and add the milk all at once.

2 Return to the heat and stir until the sauce boils and thickens. Remove from the heat. Add the prawns, lemon juice, chives, cayenne and paprika. Season with salt. Cool the mixture slightly.

3 Spoon the prawn mixture into the vol-au-vent cases, then arrange on baking trays. Bake at 200C/400F/Gas mk 6 for 10 minutes. Cool slightly before serving.

NUTRITIONAL INFORMATION	
Kcal	40
Protein	1g
Carbs	3g
Fat	3g
Salt	0.1g
Sodium	40mg

Spanish Prawns

[SERVES 4]

450 g/1 lb raw king prawns
6 tablespoons good olive oil or a
   mixture of olive and vegetable
   oil
1–2 small chillies, finely shredded
3 cloves garlic, crushed
salt
lemon wedges, to serve

TARTAR SAUCE:
6 tablespoons mayonnaise (use a
   good homemade mayonnaise if
   possible)
3 spring onions, chopped
1 tablespoon drained capers
1 tablespoon finely chopped
   gherkins
1 tablespoon chopped fresh
   parsley

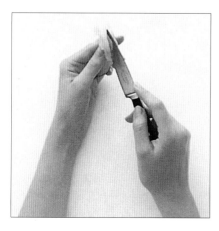

1 To prepare the tartar sauce, combine all the ingredients in a
   bowl, cover and chill until ready to serve with the seafood.

2 Peel the prawns, leaving the tail intact. Cut along the back of
   each prawn, halfway through so it curls. Remove the vein.

3 Put the oil in a frying pan and add the chillies. Heat the oil until
   very hot, then add the prawns, garlic and salt, stirring until the
prawns are bright pink. Serve immediately with crusty bread, wedges of
lemon and the tartar sauce, if desired.

NOTE: The figures given below do not include the tartar sauce. A
quarter of the sauce recipe adds 165 Kcal and 18 g of fat to each
serving.

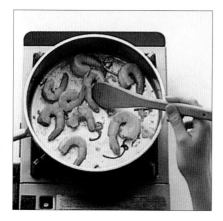

NUTRITIONAL INFORMATION	
Kcal	110
Protein	11g
Carbs	0g
Fat	7g
Salt	1.9g
Sodium	760mg

Prawns with Asian Sauce

[SERVES 4–6]

700 g/1¹/₂ lb raw king prawns
lime wedges and basil sprigs, for
  garnish

MARINADE:
handful of Thai or ordinary fresh
  basil, finely chopped
2 tablespoons finely chopped
  garlic

2 tablespoons peeled and finely
  chopped fresh ginger
2 tablespoons finely chopped
  green chillies
2 teaspoons rice wine or medium
  dry sherry
2¹/₂ tablespoons groundnut oil
1 teaspoon Chinese sesame oil
salt and pepper, to taste

1 To make the marinade, pound the ingredients together in a pestle and mortar or using the end of a rolling pin in a bowl.

2 Discard the legs and heads from the prawns then, using strong scissors, cut the prawns lengthways in half leaving the tail end intact. Remove the dark intestinal vein. Rub the marinade over the prawns, cover and leave in a cool place for 1 hour.

3 Preheat a grill or barbecue. Cook the prawns in a single layer for about 3 minutes until curled, or 'butterflied', and bright pink. Garnish with lime wedges and sprigs of basil. Serve any remaining marinade separately.

NUTRITIONAL INFORMATION	
Kcal	250
Protein	34g
Carbs	Trace
Fat	11g
Salt	6.0g
Sodium	2400mg

Baked Prawns & Courgettes

[SERVES 4]

3 courgettes, thinly sliced
  lengthways
55 g/2 oz crumbled bread, crusts
  removed
small handful of parsley, thyme,
  oregano and mint, chopped
  together
2¹/₂ tablespoons freshly grated
  Parmesan cheese

pinch of chilli powder
salt, to taste
12 raw king prawns, peeled and
  deveined
3–4 tablespoons olive oil
lemon and lime wedges, for
  garnish

1 Preheat oven to 200C/400F/Gas mk 6. Oil 4 large, individual heatproof dishes. Steam the courgette slices for 2 minutes, then set aside.

2 Mix together the bread, herbs, cheese, chilli powder and a little salt. Place a layer of courgette slices on the bottom of each dish and sprinkle with half of the bread mixture. Arrange 3 prawns in each dish, scatter over some of the bread mixture and moisten with a little olive oil.

3 Cover with courgette slices, then the remaining bread mixture. Trickle over a little oil, then cover the dishes tightly with foil. Pierce a few holes with a cocktail stick. Bake for 5–7 minutes. Serve garnished with lemon and lime wedges.

NUTRITIONAL INFORMATION	
Kcal	260
Protein	26g
Carbs	9g
Fat	13g
Salt	0.9g
Sodium	360mg

Indian-Style Prawns

[SERVES 4]

1¹/₂ tablespoons oil
1 large onion, sliced
2 cloves garlic, crushed
1–2 green chillies, seeded and
  finely chopped
1 green pepper, seeded and sliced
  or finely chopped
1-cm/¹/₂-inch piece fresh ginger,
  peeled and grated
1¹/₄ teaspoons each cumin and
  coriander seeds, toasted and
  crushed

1 teaspoon ground cinnamon
pinch of saffron threads, toasted
  and crushed
salt, to taste
700 g/1¹/₂ lb raw medium or large
  prawns, peeled
115 ml/4 fl oz plain yogurt,
  preferably strained Greek style
rice, to serve
mint leaves and yogurt, for
  garnish

1 Heat the oil in a non-stick pan. Add the onion, garlic, chilli and pepper and cook fairly gently until softened and lightly browned.

2 Stir in the ginger, cumin, coriander and cinnamon and cook over a slightly higher heat for 1–2 minutes. Add the saffron and salt, cover with water, then simmer uncovered for 20 minutes, stirring occasionally. Add the prawns and more water, if necessary, to come halfway up the prawns. Cook gently for about 4 minutes, until the prawns are cooked and turn pink.

3 Transfer the prawns to a warm plate. Boil the cooking juices over a high heat until they are syrupy. Stir a little of the juice into the yogurt, then stir back into the pan. Heat through, stirring, but do not allow to boil. Add the prawns and turn them in the sauce. Serve with rice, garnished with mint and a swirl of yogurt.

NUTRITIONAL INFORMATION	
Kcal	170
Protein	18g
Carbs	5g
Fat	10g
Salt	2.8g
Sodium	1100mg

Shrimp Risotto

[SERVES 4]

575 g/1¼ lb cooked shrimps or
 small prawns with shells
1 bouquet garni
5 black peppercorns
1 clove garlic, crushed
½ onion stuck with 1 clove
300 ml/10 fl oz medium-bodied
 dry white wine

2 shallots, finely chopped
65 g/2½ oz unsalted butter
pinch of saffron threads, toasted
 and crushed
300 g/10 oz arborio rice
2 tablespoons chopped fresh
 tarragon, plus extra for garnish
salt and pepper, to taste

1 Peel the prawns; set aside. Place the shells, bouquet garni, peppercorns, garlic, onion, wine and 1 litre/35 fl oz water in a saucepan, bring to the boil and simmer for 20 minutes. Strain, pressing hard on the shells. Measure 1¼ litres/40 fl oz stock; make up with water if necessary. Bring to the boil.

2 In a heavy-bottomed saucepan, cook the shallots in half the butter, until translucent. Stir in the saffron and rice and cook, stirring, for 1–2 minutes, until the rice is well coated and has absorbed the butter. Over a moderate heat, stir in 150 ml/5 fl oz boiling stock. Continue to cook at a steady bubble, stirring constantly, until there is no liquid and the rice is creamy. Stir in a further 150 ml/5 fl oz boiling stock.

3 Continue to cook, adding smaller amounts of stock until the rice is soft outside but firm inside, creamy and bound together, about 15–20 minutes. Add the prawns towards the end of the cooking time. Remove the pan from the heat, dice the remaining butter and stir in with the tarragon. Cover and leave for 1 minute to absorb the butter. Stir, add salt, if necessary, and serve immediately. Garnish with tarragon.

NUTRITIONAL INFORMATION	
Kcal	570
Protein	31g
Carbs	64g
Fat	15g
Salt	0.7g
Sodium	280mg

Scallop, Prawn & Mint Salad

[SERVES 6]

115 ml/4 fl oz dry white wine
1/2 onion, chopped
1 bay leaf
4 black peppercorns, crushed
450 g/1 lb small courgettes
450 g/1 lb shelled scallops
450 g/1 lb raw large prawns,
   peeled
2 tomatoes, peeled, seeded and
   chopped
about 18 small mint leaves

DRESSING:
3–4 tablespoons lime juice
1/2 teaspoon finely grated lime
   rind
1/2 clove garlic, finely chopped
115 ml/4 fl oz extra virgin olive oil
2 tablespoons chopped fresh
   parsley
salt and pepper, to taste

1 Heat the wine, onion, bay leaf and peppercorns with 550 ml/18 fl oz water in a saucepan, simmer for 15 minutes, then add the courgettes and cook for about 8 minutes, until tender but crisp. Remove the courgettes and drain on kitchen paper.

2 Add the scallops and the prawns to the pan and poach until the scallops just turn opaque, about 2 minutes, and the prawns become pink, 3–4 minutes.

3 Drain the seafood and cool under cold running water. Halve the scallops horizontally and slice the courgettes into thin strips. Place in a serving dish with the seafood, tomatoes and mint. To make the dressing, whisk the ingredients together in a small bowl or jug, pour over the salad and toss gently to coat. Cover and chill for 30 minutes before serving.

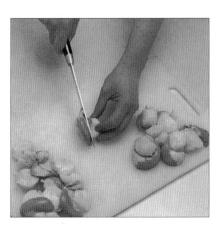

NUTRITIONAL INFORMATION	
Kcal	300
Protein	26g
Carbs	3g
Fat	19g
Salt	1.7g
Sodium	660mg

Thai Prawn & Noodle Soup

[SERVES 4]

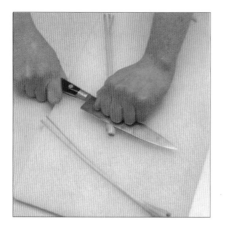

2 stalks lemon grass
425 ml/15 fl oz fish stock
2 small star anise pods
2 cloves garlic, chopped
425 ml/15 fl oz coconut milk
8 large raw prawns, shelled
4 shelled scallops, halved
   horizontally

85 g/3 oz clear vermicelli, soaked
   in cold water for 10 minutes
   then drained
2 spring onions, thinly sliced
2 fresh red chillies, seeded and
   sliced
juice of 1$\frac{1}{2}$ limes
1 tablespoon fish sauce
1 tablespoon chopped fresh
   coriander

1 Crush and chop the lemon grass stalks. Bring the stock to the boil in a large saucepan, add the lemon grass, star anise and garlic, then simmer, uncovered, for 5 minutes. Cover and leave to stand for 30 minutes.

2 Add the coconut milk to the pan and heat to simmering point. Add the prawns and scallops and poach for 1 minute.

3 Then add the vermicelli, spring onions and chillies and cook for a further minute, until the prawns are pink. Remove the pan from the heat and stir in the lime juice, fish sauce and chopped coriander. Serve immediately.

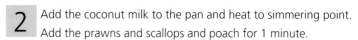

NUTRITIONAL INFORMATION	
Kcal	360
Protein	27g
Carbs	21g
Fat	18g
Salt	1.3g
Sodium	530mg

Mediterranean Fish Soup

[SERVES 6]

1.2 kg/2³/₄ lb mixed fish and
  shellfish, such as monkfish, red
  mullet, bass, bream, snapper,
  prawns, mussels, cleaned
pinch of saffron threads, toasted
  and crushed
5 tablespoons olive oil
2 Spanish onions, sliced
1 stick celery, sliced
3 cloves garlic, chopped

3 large tomatoes, peeled
bouquet garni of 1 bay leaf, sprig
  each dried thyme and fennel, 3
  parsley sprigs and a strip of
  dried orange peel
1.2 litres/2¹/₄ pints fish stock
salt and pepper, to taste
chopped fresh parsley, for garnish
French bread, to serve

1 Fillet and skin the fish (see Introduction, page 21) and cut into fairly large pieces. Remove the prawns from their shells. Soak the saffron threads in 2 tablespoons warm water for 10 minutes.

2 Heat the oil in a large saucepan. Add the onions, celery and garlic and cook gently until softened. Chop the tomatoes and add to the pan with the bouquet garni. Arrange the fish on top of the vegetables, add the saffron liquid, then pour in sufficient stock to cover the fish. Simmer, uncovered, for 6 minutes.

3 Add the shellfish and mussels to the pan and cook for a further 3–4 minutes, until the shellfish are just tender and the mussels open; discard any mussels that remain closed. Remove the bouquet garni. Season with salt and pepper. Serve garnished with parsley and accompanied by French bread.

NUTRITIONAL INFORMATION	
Kcal	270
Protein	33g
Carbs	7g
Fat	13g
Salt	0.6g
Sodium	240mg

Seafood Gumbo

[SERVES 4–6]

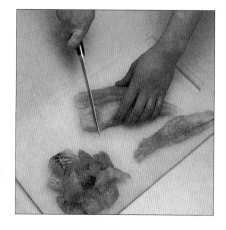

400 g/14 oz red snapper fillets or
  other firm white fish fillets
2 tablespoons olive oil
2 onions, sliced
2 cloves garlic, crushed
1 green pepper, seeded and
  chopped
1 stick celery, chopped
2 tablespoons seasoned flour
685 ml/24 fl oz fish stock
400 g/14 oz tin chopped tomatoes

85 g/3 oz cooked ham, chopped
1 bouquet garni
225 g/8 oz fresh okra, sliced
225 g/8 oz each white crabmeat
  and cooked peeled prawns
lemon juice and dash of Tabasco
  sauce
450 g/1 lb boiled long-grain rice,
  to serve
chopped fresh parsley, to serve
  (optional)

1 Cut the fish into chunks, cover and chill until required. Heat the oil in a heavy flameproof casserole. Add the onions and cook until softened. Add the garlic, pepper and celery and cook, stirring frequently, for 5 minutes.

2 Sprinkle over the flour and stir for 1 minute. Stir the stock, tomatoes, ham and bouquet garni into the casserole, partially cover and simmer for 30 minutes. Add the okra and simmer, covered, for another 30 minutes.

3 Chop the crabmeat and set aside. Add the fish to the casserole and cook for about 7 minutes. Add the crabmeat and prawns and cook for about 2^1/2 minutes, until the prawns are hot. Remove the bouquet garni. Add lemon juice and Tabasco sauce to taste. Spoon the rice into warm serving bowls and ladle the gumbo over it. Serve sprinkled with chopped fresh parsley, if liked.

NUTRITIONAL INFORMATION	
Kcal	520
Protein	52g
Carbs	49g
Fat	15g
Salt	3.8g
Sodium	1490mg

Lobster with Basil Dressing

[SERVES 4]

4 lobsters, about 450–575 g/1–1¼
    lb each, cooked (see Note)
lamb's lettuce salad, to serve
lemon wedges, to serve

DRESSING:
55 g/2 oz sun-dried tomatoes in
    olive oil, drained and chopped
1 small bunch basil, chopped
4 tablespoons walnut oil
2 tablespoons Spanish sherry
    vinegar
black pepper, to taste

1 To make the dressing, chop the tomatoes and basil together. In a bowl, whisk together the oil and vinegar and then stir in the tomatoes and basil. Season with black pepper.

2 Using a large heavy knife and working from head to tail along the back, split the lobsters in half. Remove and discard the intestine that runs through the centre of the body to the tail and the stomach from near the head.

3 Brush the cut side of the lobsters generously with the dressing and set aside for 15 minutes. Preheat the grill. Grill the lobsters for about 3 minutes. Meanwhile, gently warm the remaining dressing in a small saucepan. Brush the lobsters with the dressing and serve with a lamb's lettuce salad and lemon wedges. Serve the remaining dressing separately.

NOTE: If possible, order the lobsters from your fishmonger and ask for them to be only three-quarters cooked. Use them the same day.

NUTRITIONAL INFORMATION	
Kcal	580
Protein	80g
Carbs	3g
Fat	28g
Salt	3.0g
Sodium	1200mg

Crab & Black Bean Sauce

[SERVES 4]

700 g/1¹/₂ lb fresh whole crab, cooked (see Note)
1¹/₄ tablespoons groundnut oil
2–3 cloves garlic, crushed
3 whole spring onions, cut into 5-cm/2-inch pieces
3 (¹/₂-cm/¹/₄-inch) slices fresh ginger, peeled and chopped
2 tablespoons fermented black beans

2 fresh red chillies, seeded and thinly sliced
1¹/₄ tablespoons light soy sauce
2 tablespoons rice wine or medium sherry
115 ml/4 fl oz fish stock, preferably made from prawn shells and heads
coriander sprigs, for garnish

1 Detach the claws and legs from the crab and divide the claws at the joints. Using a sharp heavy knife, lightly crack the claws and legs so as not to damage the flesh within.

2 Place the crab on its back (tail flap towards you). Holding the shell, press the body section up from under the tail flap and ease out. Pull off the gills and discard. Cut the body into quarters. Remove the stomach bag and mouth from the back shell. Scrape out the brown meat.

3 Heat the oil in a preheated a wok or frying pan. Add the garlic, spring onions and ginger and stir-fry until fragrant. Add the beans, chillies and crab, stir-fry for 2 minutes, then add the soy sauce, rice wine and stock. Tip the mixture into a flameproof casserole, cover and cook for 5 minutes. Serve garnished with coriander.

NOTE: If possible, order a crab from your fishmongers and ask for it to be only three-quarters cooked. Use it the same day.

NUTRITIONAL INFORMATION	
Kcal	100
Protein	8g
Carbs	1g
Fat	6g
Salt	1.1g
Sodium	440mg

Crab Soufflé

[SERVES 4–6]

45 g/1¹/₂ oz butter
1 tablespoon grated onion
45 g/1¹/₂ oz plain flour
175 ml/6 fl oz milk
150 g/5 oz soft cheese
3 tablespoons chopped fresh
  parsley
1¹/₂ teaspoons anchovy essence
2–3 teaspoons lemon juice
5 eggs, separated

225 g/8 oz mixed white and
  brown crabmeat
1 egg white
salt and pepper, to taste
2 tablespoons freshly grated
  Parmesan cheese
orange and fennel salad, to serve

1 Preheat oven to 200C/400F/Gas mk 6. Place a baking tray to heat in the top third of the oven. Butter a 2¹/₄-litre/4-pint soufflé dish, or individual ramekins. In a saucepan, melt the butter, add the onion and cook for 2–3 minutes. Stir in the flour, cook for 1 minute.

2 Gradually stir in the milk. Bring to the boil, stirring, then simmer gently for 4 minutes, stirring occasionally. Remove from the heat and stir in the soft cheese, chopped parsley, anchovy essence, lemon juice, egg yolks and crab. Season with salt and pepper.

3 Whisk all the egg whites until stiff but not dry. Stir 2 tablespoons into the crab mixture, then fold in the remaining egg whites. Transfer to the soufflé dish or dishes, sprinkle the Parmesan cheese over the top and place the dish or dishes on the baking tray. Bake for 40–45 minutes, or 12–15 minutes for individual soufflés, until lightly set in the centre. Serve immediately with an orange and fennel salad.

NUTRITIONAL INFORMATION	
Kcal	420
Protein	31g
Carbs	12g
Fat	28g
Salt	1.5g
Sodium	600mg

Cajun Crabcakes

[MAKES 8]

1 small clove garlic, finely chopped
2 tablespoons finely chopped spring onions (white and green parts)
2 tablespoons finely chopped red pepper
pinch of salt
1 egg, beaten
1¹/₂ tablespoons mayonnaise
450 g/1 lb fresh white and brown crabmeat, chopped

1 tablespoon chopped fresh parsley
115 g/4 oz fresh breadcrumbs
squeeze of lemon juice
salt and cayenne pepper, to taste
olive oil, for shallow frying
sour cream, to serve
chopped chives, to serve
crisp green salad, to serve
lemon wedges, for garnish

1 Place the garlic, spring onions, pepper and a pinch salt in a mortar or small bowl and crush together using a pestle or the end of a rolling pin.

2 Transfer to a mixing bowl and stir in the egg, mayonnaise, crabmeat, parsley and about half the breadcrumbs to bind together. Add lemon juice, salt and cayenne pepper to taste.

3 Form the crab mixture into 8 cakes, 2 cm/³/4 inch thick and 6 cm/2¹/2 inches round. Lightly press in the remaining breadcrumbs. Cover and chill for 1 hour. In a non-stick frying pan, heat a thin layer of oil, add the crabcakes in batches and fry for 3–4 minutes on each side, until golden. Serve warm with sour cream and chives, a crisp green salad and lemon wedges.

NUTRITIONAL INFORMATION	
Kcal	170
Protein	14g
Carbs	7g
Fat	10g
Salt	0.8g
Sodium	300mg

Cioppino

[SERVES 4]

2 tablespoons light olive oil
1 large onion, chopped
3 cloves garlic, chopped
1 small red chilli, seeded and
 thinly sliced
1 red pepper, seeded and sliced
575 g/1¼ lb tomatoes
425 ml/15 fl oz fish stock
115 ml/4 fl oz dry white wine
1 teaspoon dried oregano
1½ teaspoons each chopped fresh
 thyme and marjoram

1 bay leaf
225 g/8 oz haddock, cod or halibut
 fillet, skinned
225 g/8 oz large raw prawns
16 mussels, cleaned (see page 22)
4 large scallops, shelled
2½ tablespoons chopped fresh
 parsley
8 cooked, unpeeled large prawns,
 for garnish (optional)

1 In a large, heavy-bottomed saucepan, heat the oil, then add the onion, garlic, chilli and red pepper. Cook gently until the onion begins to colour.

2 Meanwhile, peel, seed and chop the tomatoes. Add to the pan with the stock, wine and herbs. Cover and simmer for 45 minutes.

3 Cut the fish into cubes and peel the prawns. Add the mussels to the pan, simmer for 1 minute, then add the haddock, prawns and scallops. Cook over a low heat for 3–5 minutes, until the mussels have opened; discard any that remain closed. Sprinkle with chopped parsley and serve at once. Garnish with 8 unpeeled, cooked large prawns, if liked.

NUTRITIONAL INFORMATION	
Kcal	340
Protein	45g
Carbs	11g
Fat	11g
Salt	1.5g
Sodium	610mg

Seafood Pâté

[SERVES 10]

450 g/1 lb white fish fillets
450 g/1 lb raw prawns
85 g/3 oz butter
6 spring onions, chopped
250 g/8 oz scallops (optional)
1 clove garlic, crushed
2 tablespoons Cognac or brandy
125 ml/4 fl oz single cream
1 tablespoon lemon juice
1 teaspoon paprika
good pinch of cayenne pepper
green salad and melba toast, to
  serve

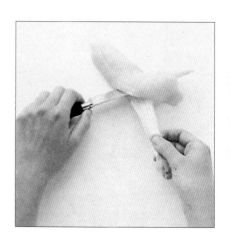

1 To remove the skin from the fish, place the fish, skin side down
and use a sharp knife to separate the flesh, pulling the skin from
side to side. Cut the fish into chunks. Peel and de-vein the prawns.

2 Melt the butter in a frying pan and gently sauté the spring
onions for 2 minutes. Add the fish, prawns, scallops (if using)
and garlic. Cook, turning until the prawns turn pink and the fish flakes.

3 Warm the Cognac, ignite and pour over the fish mixture. When
the flames subside, add the cream. Stir in the lemon juice,
paprika and cayenne. Cool. Put the mixture into a food processor and
blend. Turn the mixture into one large or several small serving dishes,
cover and chill until firm. Serve with a green salad and melba toast.

NUTRITIONAL INFORMATION	
Kcal	180
Protein	19g
Carbs	1g
Fat	11g
Salt	1.2g
Sodium	490mg

NOTE: The nutritional figures given include scallops.

Taramasalata

[SERVES 4–6]

2 thick slices of crusty bread,
  weighing about 175 g/6 oz
125 g/4 oz tarama (salted grey
  mullet roe)
1 clove garlic, crushed
1 tablespoon grated onion
1 egg yolk
2–3 tablespoons lemon juice
125 ml /4 fl oz olive oil
black olive, for garnish
crusty bread, to serve

1 Remove the crusts from the bread. Cover in cold water and soak for 10 minutes. Squeeze out the water.

2 Crumb the bread in a food processor. Remove. Place the tarama in the processor, add the garlic and onion and process until thoroughly mixed. Gradually add the breadcrumbs until the mixture is smooth. Blend in the egg yolk and 1 tablespoon of the lemon juice.

3 With the processor on, gradually pour in the olive oil, mixing until very creamy. Add more lemon juice to taste. Cover and chill. Garnish with a black olive. Serve with crusty bread for dipping.

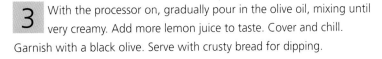

NOTE: Tarama is the salted roe from grey mullet and is available from many delicatessens and larger supermarkets. Smoked cod's roe can be substitued for the tarama if unavailable.

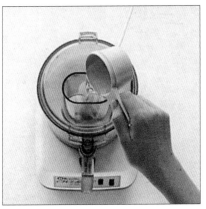

NUTRITIONAL INFORMATION	
Kcal	390
Protein	9g
Carbs	23g
Fat	30g
Salt	1.3g
Sodium	530mg

Seafood Toasts

[MAKES 24]

6 slices white bread
250 g/8 oz raw prawns
250 g/8 oz white fish fillets
2 eggs
1 tablespoon ginger wine or dry
sherry
1 tablespoon soy sauce
1/2 teaspoon salt
1 tablespoon cornflour
fresh parsley sprigs (optional)
vegetable oil, for deep-frying

1 Trim the crusts from the bread so that each slice is square. Cut each slice across the diagonal to make 4 quarters

2 Peel and de-vein the prawns. Remove any bones and skin from the fish. Put the prawns and fish into a food processor with 1 egg, the ginger wine, soy sauce, salt and cornflour. Blend to a smooth paste. Spread evenly on the pieces of bread.

3 Beat the remaining egg and brush over the spread seafood. Press a sprig of parsley on top of each. Heat the oil in a frying pan. When hot add the seafood-topped bread, a few pieces at a time. Turn triangles occasionally until golden all over. Drain and repeat until all are cooked. Serve hot or warm.

NUTRITIONAL INFORMATION	
Kcal	60
Protein	4g
Carbs	2g
Fat	4g
Salt	0.5g
Sodium	170mg

Cucumber with Mussels

[MAKES ABOUT 30]

100 g/3^1/$_2$ oz canned smoked
  mussels or oysters
1 teaspoon lemon juice
few drops of Tabasco sauce
125 g/4 oz full-fat cream cheese
3 tablespoons finely chopped
  celery
1 cucumber (use long ones with
  few seeds)
salmon roe and fresh dill sprigs,
  for garnish

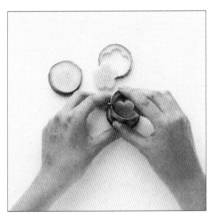

1 Drain the oil from the mussels or oysters and place them in a small bowl.

2 Add the lemon juice, Tabasco sauce and cheese. Transfer to a food processor and blend well together. Turn into a bowl and stir in the chopped celery. Cover and chill the mixture until needed. Cut the cucumber into 1-cm/^{1}/$_2$-in thick slices. Stamp out with a fluted cutter and scoop a little flesh from the centre of each.

3 Spoon some of the mussel mixture on to each cucumber slice. Garnish with salmon roe and a dill sprig. Serve immediately.

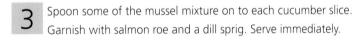

NUTRITIONAL INFORMATION	
Kcal	30
Protein	1g
Carbs	Trace
Fat	2g
Salt	Trace
Sodium	20mg

Stuffed Mussels

[SERVES 2]

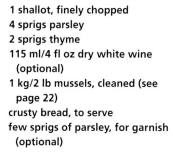

1 shallot, finely chopped
4 sprigs parsley
2 sprigs thyme
115 ml/4 fl oz dry white wine
  (optional)
1 kg/2 lb mussels, cleaned (see
  page 22)
crusty bread, to serve
few sprigs of parsley, for garnish
  (optional)

STUFFING:
1–2 cloves garlic, halved
4 sprigs parsley
leaves from 2 sprigs thyme
1 thin slice day-old bread
85 g/3 oz unsalted butter
1 teaspoon grated lemon rind
2 teaspoons lemon juice
1¼ teaspoons Dijon mustard
salt and pepper, to taste

1 Place the shallot, parsley and thyme in a large saucepan with the wine or 115 ml/4 fl oz water and simmer for a few minutes, then add the mussels. Cover, bring to the boil and cook the mussels for 4–5 minutes, shaking the pan frequently, until the shells open; discard any that remain closed.

2 To make the stuffing, chop the garlic and herbs together in a food processor or blender. Remove the crusts from the bread and add to the garlic and herbs along with the butter, lemon rind and juice, mustard and salt and pepper; set aside.

3 Preheat the grill. Discard the top shells from the mussels. Strain the cooking juices and add 2–3 teaspoons to the stuffing to moisten it. Using a teaspoon, spread a generous amount of stuffing on each mussel, then place in a shallow baking dish. Grill for about 3 minutes, until golden and bubbling. Serve with crusty bread and garnish sprigs of parsley, if liked.

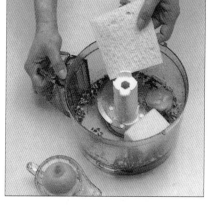

NUTRITIONAL INFORMATION	
Kcal	530
Protein	28g
Carbs	11g
Fat	39g
Salt	1.0g
Sodium	410mg

Mussels in Tomato Sauce

[SERVES 2–3]

2 tablespoons olive oil
2 shallots, finely chopped
2 cloves garlic, crushed
150 ml/5 fl oz medium-bodied dry
  white wine
250 g/9 oz tomatoes, peeled,
  seeded and chopped
finely grated rind of 1 lemon

2 tablespoons capers, chopped
3 tablespoons chopped fresh
  parsley
1¹/₂ kg/3¹/₄ lb fresh mussels,
  cleaned
salt and pepper, to taste
crusty bread, to serve

1 In a large saucepan, heat the oil, then add the shallots and garlic and cook gently until softened. Add the wine, tomatoes, lemon rind, capers and half the parsley. Bring to the boil.

2 Add the mussels to the pan, cover and cook over a high heat for 3–4 minutes or until the mussels have opened, shaking pan frequently; discard any mussels that remain closed.

3 Season with salt and pepper. Transfer to a large serving bowl or individual soup plates, sprinkle over the remaining parsley and serve with crusty bread.

NUTRITIONAL INFORMATION	
Kcal	380
Protein	41g
Carbs	8g
Fat	18g
Salt	1.5g
Sodium	590mg

Herb & Garlic Mussels

[MAKES ABOUT 30 DEPENDING ON THE SIZE OF THE MUSSELS]

1 kg/2¼ lb unshelled mussels
500 ml/16 fl oz water
125 g/4 oz butter, softened
2 cloves garlic, crushed
2 tablespoons chopped fresh
  parsley
1 tablespoon snipped fresh chives
1 tablespoon chopped fresh dill

1 Scrub the mussels well, removing the beards. Cover with cold water and soak for several hours. Discard any mussels with broken shells. Drain.

2 Bring the water to the boil in a frying pan. Add a layer of mussels and remove them once they open. Add more mussels as the cooked ones are removed. Discard any that do not open. Lift off the top shell of each mussel and discard. Beat the butter with the remaining ingredients.

3 Spread the herb butter over each of the mussels. Chill until ready to cook. Place under a hot grill until tops colour. Serve hot.

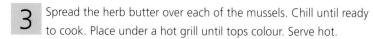

NUTRITIONAL INFORMATION	
Kcal	40
Protein	2g
Carbs	Trace
Fat	4g
Salt	0.1g
Sodium	50mg

Indonesian Steamed Mussels

[SERVES 4]

1 kg/2¹/₄ lb mussels or clams,
    cleaned
7¹/₂-cm/3-inch piece lemon grass,
    crushed and chopped
7¹/₂-cm/3-inch piece fresh ginger,
    peeled and chopped
10 sprigs basil
torn basil leaves, for garnish

SWEET AND SOUR SAUCE:
400 g/14 oz red peppers, seeded
    and chopped
55 g/2 oz fresh red chillies, seeded
    and chopped
3 cloves garlic, roughly chopped
4 tablespoons sugar
6 tablespoons vinegar
2 tablespoons olive oil
salt, to taste

1 To make the sauce, place the peppers, chillies, garlic and 2 tablespoons water into a blender and purée.

2 Transfer to a non-aluminium saucepan and add the remaining sauce ingredients with 150 ml/5 fl oz water. Bring to the boil and simmer for 20 minutes or until reduced by half. Leave to cool, then transfer to a jar and refrigerate to allow the flavours to develop. (It can be refrigerated for up to 2 weeks.)

3 Place the mussels or clams, lemon grass, ginger and basil sprigs in a large saucepan and add sufficient water to come 4 cm /1¹/₂ inches up the sides of the pan. Bring to the boil, cover and cook over a moderate heat for 3–5 minutes, until the shells have opened; discard any that are closed. Meanwhile, transfer the sauce to a small bowl. Drain the mussels or clams, garnish with torn basil leaves and serve with the sauce.

NUTRITIONAL INFORMATION	
Kcal	220
Protein	14g
Carbs	23g
Fat	8g
Salt	0.4g
Sodium	160mg

Oysters Rockefeller

[SERVES 4]

few handfuls of rock salt
24 oysters, opened, on the half
  shell
115 g/4 oz butter
2 shallots, finely chopped
1 stick celery, finely chopped
225 g/8 oz spinach, finely chopped
1 tablespoon chopped fresh
  parsley

1½ teaspoons chopped fresh
  tarragon
2 tablespoons fresh breadcrumbs
1 tablespoon Pernod or pastis
dash of Tabasco sauce and
  Worcestershire sauce
salt and pepper, to taste
lemon slices, to serve (optional)
sprigs of parsley, for garnish
  (optional)

1 Spread a generous layer of rock salt over the bottom of a grill pan. Nestle the oysters in the salt.

2 In a saucepan or frying pan, heat a quarter of the butter, add the shallots and celery. Cook gently, until softened but not coloured. Stir in the spinach, parsley and tarragon and cook over a moderate heat until the surplus moisture from the spinach has evaporated.

3 Preheat the grill. Purée the spinach mixture in a blender, then mix in the breadcrumbs, remaining butter, Pernod or pastis, Tabasco and Worcestershire sauces and season with salt and pepper. Place a tablespoonful of spinach mixture on each oyster and grill for about 3 minutes, until beginning to turn golden. Serve at once with lemon slices and sprigs of parsley, if liked.

NUTRITIONAL INFORMATION	
Kcal	280
Protein	9g
Carbs	6g
Fat	25g
Salt	1.7g
Sodium	650mg

Oysters with Caviar

[MAKES 36]

36 oysters on the shell
2 tablespoons thick mayonnaise or
   sour cream
salt and pepper
squeeze of lemon juice
1 teaspoon tomato paste
2 teaspoons bottled horseradish
   or to taste
3–4 tablespoons black caviar
fresh dill sprigs, for garnish

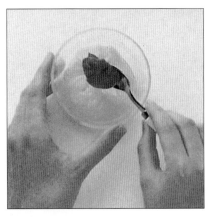

1 Arrange the oysters on serving dishes and sit the dishes on ice.

2 Season the mayonnaise with salt and pepper and stir in a squeeze of lemon juice and the tomato paste. Add the horseradish. The sauce should have a definite taste of horseradish so add more if needed.

3 Spoon a little of this sauce onto each oyster. Top with the caviar and garnish with a dill sprig. Alternatively, the sauce may be served in a separate bowl with the caviar alongside for spooning over the oysters.

NUTRITIONAL INFORMATION	
Kcal	20
Protein	2g
Carbs	Trace
Fat	1g
Salt	0.2g
Sodium	60mg

Angels on Horseback

[MAKES 8]

4 bacon slices, rinds removed
8 oysters, shucked
4 slices bread
unsalted butter, for spreading
freshly ground black pepper, to
  taste
lamb's lettuce and lemon twists,
  for garnish

1 Preheat the grill. Cut each bacon slice across in half, then stretch each piece with the back of a knife. Wrap a piece of bacon around each oyster.

2 Place on a grill rack with the ends of bacon underneath. Toast the bread, then place the oysters under the grill until crisp, turn over and crisp the other side.

3 Meanwhile, cut 2 circles from each slice of toast and butter the circles. Place an oyster on each circle, grind over black pepper and serve garnished with lamb's lettuce and lemon twists.

NUTRITIONAL INFORMATION	
Kcal	130
Protein	5g
Carbs	9g
Fat	8g
Salt	1.0g
Sodium	380mg

Oysters in Beds

[SERVES 2]

2 miniature brioches
55 g/2 oz unsalted butter, melted
6 large oysters
4 tablespoons sour cream
cayenne pepper and white pepper,
  to taste
shredded lemon rind and slices,
  for garnish
tomato, onion and tarragon salad,
  to serve

1 Preheat oven to 220C/425F/Gas mk 7. Remove the top knobs from the brioches. Scoop out the insides to leave a thin shell, taking care not to pierce the walls. Brush the brioche shells inside and out with half of the melted butter. Place on a baking tray and bake for 5–10 minutes, until crisp.

2 Meanwhile, scrub the oysters then, holding one at a time, curved side down in a cloth, prise open the shells at the hinge using a strong, shortbladed knife. Loosen each oyster and pour the liquid into the pan with the remaining melted butter. Boil for a few minutes until liquid is reduced then, over a low heat, add the sour cream. Heat gently without boiling. Season with cayenne and white pepper.

3 Place 3 oysters in each brioche and pour the sauce over them. Garnish with lemon rind and slices and serve with a tomato, onion and tarragon salad.

NUTRITIONAL INFORMATION	
Kcal	360
Protein	7g
Carbs	11g
Fat	33g
Salt	0.6g
Sodium	250mg

SMOKED FISH

Kedgeree

[SERVES 4]

575 g/1¼ lb smoked haddock or salmon
115 g/4 oz long grain rice
2 tablespoons lemon juice
150 ml/5 fl oz single or sour cream
pinch of freshly grated nutmeg
pinch of cayenne pepper, plus extra for garnish (optional)
2 hard-boiled eggs, peeled and chopped
55 g/2 oz butter, diced
2 tablespoons chopped fresh parsley
parsley sprigs and sliced hard-boiled eggs, for garnish

1 Place the fish in a saucepan, just cover with water and poach for about 10 minutes. Lift the fish from the cooking liquid, discard the bones and skin and flake the flesh. Measure the cooking liquid to twice the volume of rice; top up with water if necessary.

2 Bring to the boil, add the rice, stir, then cover and simmer for 15 minutes, until the rice is tender and the liquid has been absorbed. Meanwhile, preheat oven to 180C/350F/Gas mk 4 and butter a baking dish. Remove the rice from the heat.

3 Stir in the lemon juice, cream, fish, nutmeg and a pinch of cayenne. Gently fold in the eggs. Turn into the prepared dish, dot with butter and bake for 25 minutes. Stir in the chopped parsley and garnish with parsley sprigs and hard-boiled egg. Sprinkle cayenne pepper over the top, if liked.

NUTRITIONAL INFORMATION	
Kcal	470
Protein	41g
Carbs	25g
Fat	23g
Salt	4.9g
Sodium	1920mg

Haddock in Jacket Potatoes

[SERVES 4]

4 large baking potatoes, scrubbed
  and pricked with a fork
450 g/1 lb smoked haddock
200 ml/7 fl oz milk
2–3 teaspoons lemon juice
black pepper, to taste
5–6 tablespoons sour cream or

plain yogurt, preferably Greek
  style
2 tablespoons chopped fresh
  chives
1 tablespoon chopped fresh
  parsley salad, to serve
mixed salad, to serve (optional)

1 Preheat oven to 200C/400F/Gas mk 6. Bake the potatoes for 1^1/$_2$ hours until tender.

2 Meanwhile, place the fish in a baking dish, pour over the milk, cover with greaseproof paper and cook on the bottom shelf in the oven for about 8 minutes, until the flesh flakes. Drain the fish, reserving the milk. Flake the flesh finely, discarding the skin and bones, and season with lemon juice and pepper. In a small bowl, mix the sour cream or yogurt with the chives, parsley and season with pepper.

3 Cut a slice from the top of each potato. Scoop out most of the insides of the potatoes into a bowl, taking care not to pierce the skins. Beat the potato insides with the reserved milk and pepper to taste, then·mix in the flaked fish. Spoon the fish mixture back into the potato skins and spoon half of the sour cream or yogurt over the top. Return to the oven for about 10 minutes. Pour over the remaining cream or yogurt and serve with a mixed salad, if liked.

NUTRITIONAL INFORMATION	
Kcal	360
Protein	34g
Carbs	46g
Fat	6g
Salt	3.6g
Sodium	1430mg

Omelette Arnold Bennett

[SERVES 2]

175 g/6 oz smoked haddock fillet, poached and flaked
55 g/2 oz butter, diced
175 ml/6 fl oz whipping cream
4 eggs, separated

black pepper, to taste
65 g/2½ oz grated mature Cheddar cheese
mixed leaf salad, to serve

1 Discard the skin and bones from the fish and flake the flesh. In a fairly small non-stick saucepan, melt half of the butter in 4 tablespoons cream, then gently stir in the fish. Cover, remove from the heat and leave to cool.

2 Stir together the egg yolks, 1 tablespoon cream and pepper, then gently stir in the fish mixture. In a separate bowl, stir together the cheese and remaining cream. Preheat the grill. Whisk the egg whites until stiff but not dry, then lightly fold into the fish mixture in 3 batches.

3 In an omelette pan, heat the remaining butter. Pour in the fish mixture and cook until set and lightly browned underneath, but still quite moist on the top. Pour the cheese mixture over the omelette, then grill until golden and bubbling. Serve with a mixed leaf salad.

NUTRITIONAL INFORMATION	
Kcal	940
Protein	46g
Carbs	3g
Fat	82g
Salt	4.3g
Sodium	1700mg

Smoked Salmon Scramble

[SERVES 2]

115 g/4 oz smoked salmon
  trimmings, chopped
2 tablespoons single cream
45 g/1¹/₂ oz unsalted butter
4 large eggs, beaten
black pepper, to taste
chopped fresh chives and lime
  slices, for garnish
buttered toasted bagels, muffins
  or crumpets, to serve (optional)

1 In a small bowl, mix the smoked salmon and cream together. Leave to stand for 10–15 minutes.

2 In a saucepan, melt half of the butter, then stir in the eggs. Cook over a low heat, stirring with a wooden spoon, until beginning to set. Add the salmon and cream and season with pepper. Continue to stir until the eggs are almost set.

3 Remove the pan from the heat and immediately stir in the remaining butter. Garnish with chopped chives and lime slices and serve with buttered toasted bagels, muffins or crumpets.

NUTRITIONAL INFORMATION	
Kcal	470
Protein	32g
Carbs	1g
Fat	38g
Salt	3.3g
Sodium	1300mg

Smoked Salmon Quiches

[MAKES 24]

1/2 (375-g/12-oz) packet frozen
  puff pastry, defrosted
6 eggs
375 ml/12 fl oz heavy (thickened)
  cream
1/2 teaspoon salt
pinch of grated nutmeg
125 g/4 oz finely chopped smoked
  salmon
black caviar, extra salmon and dill
  sprigs, for garnish

1 Roll out the pastry thinly. Cut into 24 rounds with a 6^{1}/2-cm/2^{1}/2-inch cutter. Line greased patty tins with the pastry rounds.

2 Beat the eggs with the cream, salt and nutmeg until well mixed. Stir in the salmon. Spoon the mixture into the pastry cases, ensuring the salmon is evenly distributed.

3 Bake at 200C/400F/Gas mk 6 for 10–15 minutes or until puffed and golden. Serve warm.

NOTE: For large parties, the quiches may be cooked in advance, removed from the tins and chilled. To re-heat, place on flat trays and warm at 200C/400F/Gas mk 6 for 5 minutes.

NUTRITIONAL INFORMATION	
Kcal	140
Protein	4g
Carbs	3g
Fat	12g
Salt	0.5g
Sodium	200mg

Index